SALARY SURVEYS AND ANTITRUST

~

AN OVERVIEW FOR THE HR PROFESSIONAL

By John Davis, Ph.D., CCP

ACKNOWLEDGMENTS

I owe a debt of gratitude to many people for this report.

I want to thank the many compensation practitioners and consulting firms who participated in the WorldatWork survey regarding salary surveys. Their input provided valuable information regarding prevailing policies and practices of surveys. The attorneys, who wished to remain anonymous, were very generous to share their insights into this controversial subject. The research librarians at Southern Methodist University and the University of Texas at Dallas helped locate hard-to-find references.

The editors and writers at WorldatWork took a rather lengthy and detailed manuscript and transformed it into a readable and understandable document, and the constructive comments of the reviewers helped keep the focus of the report. Finally, I want to thank WorldatWork and its staff who so enthusiastically supported this study, and in particular Ryan Johnson, who helped guide the research and directed the survey among the WorldatWork membership. Without his guidance and support, this study would not have come to fruition.

EDITORIAL
Andrea Healey
Dan Cafaro
Ryan Johnson
Rodney Platt

TECHNICAL REVIEWERS
David A. Pierson, Ph.D., The Pierson Group
Mark E. Pittel, CCP, Sullivan Cotter & Associates Inc.
Robert M. Skladany, Welleseley Consulting Group
Laura Thanasse, CCP, CBP, GRP, Chrysalis Group

TECHNICAL REVIEW COORDINATOR
Betty Laurie

PRODUCTION MANAGER
Rebecca Williams Ficker

DESIGN
Kris Sotelo

WorldatWork is the world's leading not-for-profit professional association dedicated to knowledge leadership in compensation, benefits and total rewards. Founded in 1955, WorldatWork focuses on disciplines associated with attracting, retaining and motivating employees. In addition to providing professional affiliation, WorldatWork offers highly acclaimed certification (CCP®, CBP™ and GRP®) and education programs, the monthly *workspan*® magazine, online information resources, surveys, publications, conferences, research and networking opportunities.

WorldatWork • 14040 N. Northsight Blvd., Scottsdale, AZ 85260
480/922-2020 • Fax 480/483-8352 • www.worldatwork.org

© 2003 WorldatWork
ISBN: 1-57963-1509

Any laws, regulations or other legal requirements noted in this publication are, to the best of our knowledge, accurate and current as of this book's publishing date. We are providing this information with the understanding that WorldatWork is not engaged, directly or by implication, in rendering legal, accounting or other related professional services. You are urged to consult with an attorney, accountant or other qualified professional concerning your own specific situation and any questions that you may have related to that.
No portion of this publication may be reproduced in any form without express written permission from WorldatWork.

TABLE OF CONTENTS

TABLE OF CONTENTS iii

EXECUTIVE SUMMARY 1

INTRODUCTION 5

CHAPTER 1: HISTORY, ENFORCEMENT
AND CASE LAW 9
- Antitrust Origins 10
- Enforcing Antitrust 11
- Case History 12

CHAPTER 2: SAFE HARBOR GUIDELINES 15
- Antitrust Safety Zone (Safe Harbor) 16

CHAPTER 3: PRACTICAL AND STATISTICAL
IMPLICATIONS OF COMPLIANCE 19
- Age of Data 20
- Matching a Job 21
- Percent of a Single Statistic 21
- Basic Statistics 22
- Single Sampling of One Company 24
- Figure 1: Dominant Company Pays Low 24
- Percentiles 25
- Figure 2: Dominant Company Pays in the Middle 25
- Figure 3: Dominant Company Pays High 26

- Single Sampling of More than One Company 26
- Figure 4: Two Dominant Companies Pay High............................27
- Iterative Sampling 27
- Figure 5: Two Dominant Companies Pay High, Iterative Sampling 28
- Figure 6: Two Dominant Companies Pay Low, Iterative Sampling 29
- Which Measure to Use? 30
  - Weighted Average..30
  - Unweighted Average 30
  - Combination Average 30
  - Median 31
- Distribution of Data for 10 Jobs 32
- Year-to-Year Trends 33
- Summary of Statistical Implications...34
- Figure 7: Trends from One Year to the Next 34

CHAPTER 4: COMPENSATION PRACTITIONERS AND SALARY SURVEY PRACTICES 37

- Figure 8: Size of Participating Organizations..............................39
- Salary Surveys Conducted by Third Parties 39
- Figure 9: Number of Third Party Surveys Participated in During Previous 12 Months 40
- Elaboration on Minimum Number of Matches............................40
- Figure 10: Responses Concerning Guidelines, Matches and Dominance..41
- Elaboration on Maximum Domination of a Company 42

- Salary Surveys Not Conducted by Consultants
  or Other Third Parties 42
- Figure 11: Number of Non-Third Party Surveys Participated
  in During Previous 12 Months 43
- Figure 12: Formal or Written Guidelines
  for Non-Third Party Surveys 43
- Figure 13: Data Exchange for Non-Third Party Surveys 43
- Figure 14: Prevalence of Types and Sizes of Non-Third Party Surveys....44
- Safe Harbor Guidelines 44
- Figure 15: Familiarity with Safe Harbor Guidelines 44
- Statistical Validity..45
- Figure 16: Reliability and Validity..46

CHAPTER 5: SALARY SURVEY PRACTICES AMONG CONSULTING FIRMS 49

- Number of Surveys Conducted 50
- Number of Jobs Surveyed 51
- Minimum Number of Companies Matching a Job to Report Results 51
- Fugure 17: Minimum Number of Incumbents to Report Percentiles.......51
- Maximum Dominance Allowed
  for a Company to Report the Results 52
- Adjusting for Dominance 53
  - Surveys with Starting Data of Number
    of Incumbents and Average Pay 53
  - Surveys with Starting Data of Individual Incumbent Salaries 54
  - Serial Sampling 54
  - Stratified Sampling 55
  - Random Sampling...55
  - Other 56

- Impact of Complying with Safe Harbor 56
  - Minimum Number of Companies 56
  - Dominance 56
- Issues 56

CHAPTER 6: THE VIEWS OF ATTORNEYS 59
- Attorney No. 1 60
- Attorney No. 2 60
- Attorney No. 3 60
- Attorney No. 4 61

CHAPTER 7: SUMMARY 63
- Antitrust 64
- Safe Harbor 64
- Survey Practices of Practitioners 65
- Survey Practices of Consulting Firms 65
- Attorneys' Views 66

CHAPTER 8: NEXT STEPS 67

REFERENCES 71

APPENDICES 73
- Appendix 1: Safe Harbor Guidelines 74
- Appendix 2: Sherman Antitrust Act 79
- Appendix 3: Conflicting Views of Antitrust 82

EXECUTIVE SUMMARY

EXECUTIVE SUMMARY

In August 1996, the U.S. Department of Justice (DOJ) and the Federal Trade Commission (FTC) jointly published "Statements of Antitrust Enforcement Policy in Health Care." In these guidelines, it is suggested that salary surveys that meet certain criteria will, under most circumstances, be safe from government antitrust prosecution. The criteria indicate that surveys should contain data that is at least three months old, data that has at least five companies reporting information upon which each disseminated statistic is based, and data in which no individual participant's information represents more than 25 percent of each disseminated statistic. According to the guidelines, absent extraordinary circumstances, a salary survey that meets these criteria will be in a "safe harbor" of antitrust protection. While operating outside these rules is not automatically illegal, it could be evaluated for anticompetitive effect, if challenged.

Although the joint statements were specifically written for the exchange of information among health care providers, the so-called antitrust "safe harbor" guidelines incorporated in the statements have been adopted by an increasing number of companies outside of health care. Indeed, the 1996 antitrust statements seem to be substantially and increasingly affecting how compensation professionals gather and analyze pay data.

Unfortunately, the compensation practitioner many times is left confused. Antitrust is controversial. Some see it as preserving competition and protecting consumers; others view it as being based on flawed economic assumptions and a destroyer of free markets and property rights. This study reveals that both practitioners who use the data and the consulting firms that conduct the salary surveys vary their approach in ameliorating antitrust concerns. Also, corporate attorneys vary in their degree of caution and talk about "continuums of risk."

In addition, there are both obvious and not-so-obvious implications of compliance with safe harbor guidelines. On the more-obvious side, conforming to the requirement for three-month-old data instantly makes evergreen surveys (e.g., online surveys with current data) less fresh and, therefore, less attractive. The requirement for a minimum number of participating companies simply eliminates information on those jobs with few matches.

On the less-obvious side, the statistical effect of complying with the 25-percent maximum allowable dominance can set the adjusted weighed average off by more than 15 percent from the unadjusted value, and the behavior of the percentiles based on the adjusted data is very erratic compared with those based on the original data. In many cases, complying with safe harbor rules can give missing, false or misleading market information upon which to base compensation program decisions.

More than half of the companies surveyed in September 2002 by WorldatWork indicated that they do not have guidelines — formal or informal — regarding survey participation or use. More than one-third of those responding companies require a minimum number of matches for a job, while a slightly lower percentage require a maximum allowable dominance for a job. While virtually all of the companies participate in third-party surveys, more than 60 percent also participate in direct data exchanges. (More about this survey and its results is discussed in Chapter 4.)

This study was undertaken precisely because of this confusion, and because many organizations in a variety of industries are becoming more aware of and attempting to comply with these often-confusing guidelines. With the information presented here, compensation and human resources professionals will be better armed to make informed decisions appropriate for their organizations.

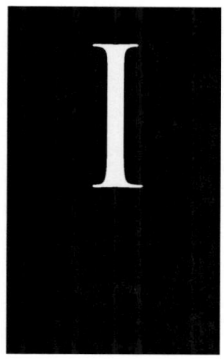

INTRODUCTION

INTRODUCTION

A survey firm conducting an annual industry salary survey received a call from a participant who had provided data for many years. The participant said his company could no longer participate unless the survey conformed to certain rules called "Safe Harbor Guidelines," one of which said that no one company could have more than 25 percent of the data in any one job. The prospective survey respondent said his company's legal department had mandated this request to minimize antitrust concerns. Not completely understanding the full implications, the survey administrator agreed to what appeared to be an innocuous request.

For each job with a dominance issue, the data of the dominant company was sampled to bring their participation rate down to no more than 25 percent. Some companies dominated certain jobs while other companies dominated other jobs; in the end, more than half the jobs in the survey were affected. When the survey results were reported back, participants were shocked. Because the participants were very familiar with the historical patterns of salary growth for the jobs, the erratic and seemingly erroneous results were immediately obvious. The pay for some jobs in a tight market reportedly declined and, for others, the increases were unrealistic. Some participants were outraged and said the survey results could not be used for compensation program decisions.

What happened? How could so-called "guidelines" wreak such havoc with statistical validity? Simply stated, the 1996 antitrust guidelines were not designed with statistical validity in mind. Instead, they were designed to minimize potential antitrust activity by companies and subsequent lawsuits.

Three recent cases, *Hoge v. Exxon Mobil Corp.*, *Todd v. Exxon Corp.*, and *Ryan, et. al. v. Amoco Corp.*, have raised antitrust awareness and concern in the compensation field. In these cases, the employees allege the employers involved violated the Sherman Antitrust Act by sharing salary information regarding certain employees, then agreeing to use that information to set the salaries of those employees at artificially low levels.

With the threat of lawsuits on the one hand and survey results that may not make sense on the other, how should compensation practitioners proceed to obtain valid market information upon which to base compensation program decisions? Do they have full information with which to make a sound decision?

With these questions and what seems to be a growing concern regarding whether to — and how to — comply with the Safe Harbor Guidelines, WorldatWork and Davis Consulting embarked upon a study of salary surveys and antitrust issues. The objective was to gather and present compensation and benefits professionals with a spectrum of information to enable them and their companies to make better and more informed decisions concerning surveys. While this report focuses on salary surveys, the same principles and perspectives apply to the exchange of information in any human resource function, whether salaries (and all forms of compensation and rewards), benefits, policies or practices.

HISTORY, ENFORCEMENT
AND CASE LAW

HISTORY, ENFORCEMENT AND CASE LAW

The DOJ/FTC Safe Harbor Guidelines are based on antitrust laws and notions. As such, it is important to have some knowledge of the antitrust laws themselves, including their origins and recent case law, to gain a perspective when making decisions regarding Safe Harbor. In addition to the brief history and summary of antitrust that follows, more detail is provided in the Appendix.

Antitrust Origins

The Sherman Antitrust Act of 1890, as amended, prohibits every contract, combination or conspiracy in restraint of trade and allows for the imposition of substantial penalties for violations thereof. Named after Sen. John Sherman, the act was proposed to address growing concern over the rapidly increasing prominence of large corporations, corporate trusts and business combinations in the U.S. economic landscape toward the end of the 19th century. Set forth as Title 15, §§ 1-7 of the U.S. Code, the Sherman Act is based on Congress' constitutional power to regulate interstate commerce and was enacted at a time when the only similar laws were state statutes governing intrastate businesses.

Though the Sherman Act had immediate potential to aid the federal government in addressing concerns over increasing corporate power, its potential was not realized for several years. Initially, Supreme Court decisions effectively prevented its use by the federal government. Thereafter, Congress gradually put in place the supporting legislation and agencies necessary to successfully challenge anticompetitive activities. This building process began in 1904 when President Theodore Roosevelt launched his "trust-busting" campaigns and the Supreme Court found in favor of the federal government, dissolving the Northern Securities Company.

The Sherman Act's reach increased during the Taft and Wilson administrations with the enactment of the Clayton Antitrust Act and the establishment of the Federal Trade Commission in 1914. Further, the addition of supplementary legislation, such as the Robinson-Patman Act during President Franklin Delano Roosevelt's administration, continued to improve the federal government's ability to challenge corporate actions on antitrust grounds. Finally, as federal antitrust agencies began broadening their interpretations of the antitrust statutes in the 1980s and 1990s, antitrust enforcement reached new heights, beginning with the 1982 breakup of the AT&T monopoly and culminating with the widely publicized Microsoft case, which ended in 2002.[1]

Virtually since its inception, antitrust has been controversial. Proponents have seen it as a preserver of competition and a protector of consumers, while critics have viewed it as being based on flawed economic assumptions and as a destroyer of free markets and property rights. The Appendix includes a summary of these conflicting views.

Although the law prohibits contracts or conspiracies that result in trade restraint, the specific practices that are illegal are not spelled out in the law. Instead, they are left to the courts to decide, based on the facts and circumstances of each case. For example, the Supreme Court decided long ago that contracts or agreements that restrain trade "unreasonably" are prohibited, with the definition of "unreasonable" being left to the courts to decide. Some practices, such as price fixing, have been declared unreasonable per se.

Enforcing Antitrust

Antitrust enforcement primarily is handled by two government agencies: the Antitrust Division of the Justice Department and the FTC. The DOJ concerns itself primarily with "conspiracies," "monopolies" and the like, while the FTC directs its attention to "unfair trade practices" in pricing, sales practices, etc.

These two antitrust organizations operate in a somewhat different fashion. The DOJ by itself cannot issue an order to impose a penalty. It must initiate a suit through the courts. The defendant may demand a jury trial. The FTC, however, is an autonomous administrative agency: it is complainant, judge, jury and prosecutor all in one, and it can issue its own cease-and-desist orders. At no time is there a jury trial in an FTC procedure.

In either type of antitrust action, the defendant may appeal the verdict to higher courts. However, in a case that may involve thousands of pieces of evidence in the form of vouchers, receipts, purchase orders, etc., the courts tend increasingly to rely on "expert" government testimony as to what is "unfair" or "monopolistic." The Supreme Court, in particular, usually upholds the government's case.

Case History

Case law and lawsuits related specifically to antitrust behavior in salary surveys date back to at least 1976. These lawsuits allege that exchanges of salary survey information under certain circumstances enable collusion among participants to keep wages artificially low. Two of the early lawsuits related specifically to salary surveys:

Women Organized for Employment filed a suit in San Francisco in 1976. The complaint alleged that the annual salary survey conducted for its 350 members by the Federated Employers of the Bay Area was used to keep the wages and benefits of the 48 clerical jobs surveyed below competitive levels. However, the case never went to court and was settled in 1977 with minimal damages.[2]

In 1982, the Massachusetts State attorney general investigated the salary survey practices of the Boston Survey Group. Again, the issue under attack was the use of an annual salary survey by the 34 association members to ostensibly hold down wage rates in a variety of clerical jobs held primarily by women. In this case, rather than being quietly settled out of court with the plaintiff recovering only minimal damages, the Boston Survey Group agreed to enter into a consent decree with the attorney general that significantly altered some of the group's survey practices. The stipulation included that each participant's input would not be identified; only aggregated information for each participant would be reported; no data would be published on a per-industry basis; any classification with fewer than 10 incumbents would not be reported; and participants may choose to allow their employees to see the aggregated survey results for their own jobs. The group also had to provide the Department of the Attorney General with a letter stating it had not and would not exchange information regarding future wage and salary plans.[3]

A third case resulted in a consent decree in the early 1990s, ending a nearly three-year federal investigation of alleged antitrust violations among nine Salt Lake City-area hospitals and health care systems, the Utah Society for Healthcare Human Resource Administration and the Utah Hospital Association. Exchange of pay data for nurses was the main compensation issue, but there also were other, non-compensation issues investigated. No charges ever were filed, but a final judgment was issued in October 1994. The decrees were for a length of five years and included:

- Prohibition of exchanging information or agreeing to exchange information directly with any other health care facility concerning the current or prospective compensation paid to nurses

- Surveys could only disseminate aggregate data from a number of participants sufficiently large enough so data could not be identified with any particular health care facility or health care facility chain.
- Representatives, agents or employees of any health care facility in Utah (excluding the third party conducting the survey) would not have access to any disaggregated data produced in response to any request for information in connection with the survey.
- If a majority of health care facilities that participated in the survey operated or had headquarters in Utah, the survey could not identify the facilities that participated in the survey or disseminate entry-level rates for a particular position, and could only disseminate the average pay rate for that position.
- Prohibition of the two named associations from conducting or facilitating any exchange or discussion among hospitals concerning current or prospective compensation paid to nurses. Historical compensation could be discussed if a written log or audiovisual recording of the exchange or discussion was made.
- The defendants were required to institute comprehensive antitrust compliance programs, designate an "antitrust compliance officer" and submit annual written certifications regarding decree compliance throughout the five-year term of the decrees.[4,5]

It is unclear whether there is a relationship between the investigation and consent decrees in Utah and the 1996 issuance of the DOJ/FTC Statements of Antitrust Enforcement Policy in Health Care from which the Safe Harbor Guidelines originated. However, the timing and content of the two events overlap, so it seems reasonable to believe that the initial investigation may have triggered or influenced the statements.

A fourth important case is *Verdin, et. al. v.R&B Falcon Drilling, et. al.*, in which more than a dozen offshore drilling companies in Houston were accused of wage fixing. The case was settled out of court in 2001 for a total of $75 million.[6] Because none of these four cases actually went to court, it cannot be said that any organization actually was guilty of any wrongdoing.

Similar to the Verdin case, three recent and important cases also involve the oil industry: *Hoge v. Exxon Mobil Corp. (District of New Jersey), Todd v. Exxon Corp., et. al. (Southern District of New York),* and *Ryan, et. al. v. Amoco Corp., et. al. (Eastern District of Texas)*. These suits were centralized in one suit by the Judicial Panel on Multidistrict Litigation and assigned to the District of New Jersey on June 19, 2002.[7] As of this writing, the suit, which is captioned "In Re Compensation of Managerial, Professional and Technical Employees Antitrust Litigation," still is active.

Some of the reasoning behind these suits is illustrated in the decision of the U.S. Court of Appeals for the Second Circuit in the aforementioned *Todd v. Exxon Corp., et. al.*, which remanded it back to the lower court for further consideration.[8] This 38-page decision is highly recommended for those who want to become familiar with the type of arguments that are made in such a suit.

SAFE HARBOR GUIDELINES

SAFE HARBOR GUIDELINES

In August 1996, the DOJ and FTC issued Statements of Antitrust Enforcement Policy in Health Care. These were first promulgated in September 1993, and have since been revised.[9] The complete text of the guidelines as they relate to salary surveys is provided in the Appendix. The most relevant extracts are presented in the following sidebar. Throughout this report, the terms "Antitrust Safety Zone" and "Safe Harbor" are used synonymously.

> **Antitrust Safety Zone (Safe Harbor)**
>
> The agencies will not challenge, absent extraordinary circumstances, provider participation in written surveys of (a) prices for health care services, or (b) wages, salaries or benefits of health care personnel, if the following conditions are satisfied:
>
> - The survey is managed by a third party (e.g., a purchaser, government agency, health care consultant, academic institution or trade association).
>
> - The information provided by survey participants is based on data more than three months old.
>
> - There are at least five providers reporting data upon which each disseminated statistic is based, no individual provider's data represents more than 25 percent on a weighted basis of that statistic, and any information disseminated is sufficiently aggregated such that it would not allow recipients to identify the prices charged or compensation paid by any particular provider.
>
> The conditions that must be met for an information exchange among providers to fall within the antitrust safety zone are intended to ensure that an exchange of price or cost data is not used by competing providers for discussion or coordination of provider prices or costs. They represent a careful balancing of a provider's individual interest in obtaining changing market conditions against the risk that the exchange of such information may permit competing providers to communicate

Antitrust Safety Zone (Safe Harbor) (continued)

with each other regarding a mutually acceptable level of prices for health care services or compensation.

Analysis of Information Exchanges that Fall Outside the Safety Zone

Exchanges of price and cost information that fall outside the antitrust safety zone generally will be evaluated to determine whether the information exchange may have an anticompetitive effect that outweighs any pro-competitive justification of the exchange. Depending on the circumstances, public-, nonprovider-initiated surveys may not raise competitive concerns. Such surveys could allow purchasers to have useful information they can use for pro-competitive purposes.

Exchanges of future prices for provider services or future compensation of employees are very likely to be considered anti-competitive. If an exchange among competing providers of price or costs information results in an agreement among competitors as to the price for the health care services or wages to be paid to health care employees, that agreement will be considered unlawful per se.

PRACTICAL AND STATISTICAL IMPLICATIONS OF COMPLIANCE

PRACTICAL AND STATISTICAL IMPLICATIONS OF COMPLIANCE

This chapter provides detail on some of the surprising, and sometimes negative, statistical effects associated with complying with the Safe Harbor guidelines to help the rewards practitioner understand the possible adverse statistical implications of adherence to the guidelines.

As noted in Chapter 2, an antitrust "safety zone" can be established through the use of data that comply with all of the following, extracted from the DOJ/FTC guidelines[9]:

- Information provided by survey participants is based on data more than three months old.

- There are at least five providers reporting data upon which each disseminated statistic is based.

- No individual provider's data represents more than 25 percent on a weighted basis of that statistic.

Age of Data

The first requirement, that the data be at least three months old, is potentially problematic for compensation survey users for several reasons. It is perhaps most troubling for today's so-called "evergreen" surveys. In recent years, more surveys are using Internet-based technology to allow participants to upload current data to an electronic survey database, then download reports or data based on current data in the database. These are known as "evergreen" surveys and they are a product both of technology (i.e., the Internet) and practitioners' needs.

Good decision-making always should be assisted by good and current data. In today's rapid-change environment — especially for jobs that are in a fast-moving market — the market price for a specific skill set or job is capable of astoundingly significant change during a short period, even as short as three months. As such, conforming to the three-month-old requirement may force a company to unwittingly use information that already may be somewhat dated.

The requirement also raises a definitional issue: how the three months is calculated. Suppose a company gives a merit increase on Dec. 1, a survey collects data "effective Jan. 1," and the survey results are made available March 1. Is the survey data two months old (January to March) or three months old (December to March)? And what about companies where the dates of increases are unknown? If the data in the survey are considered only two months old when published March 1, but a practitioner does not actually use the results until after April 1, has the three-month requirement been satisfied? Obviously, there can be more than one answer to the "simple" question concerning the data's age.

For the majority of traditional paper surveys and mostly static jobs and markets, the three-month requirement is barely a concern. But, for the newer and increasing number of so-called "evergreen" surveys that are conducted electronically, it is a concern. Further, the definitional issues around the three-month period can provide ambiguity at a minimum and antitrust exposure at the worst.

Matching a Job

Conforming to the requirement of a minimum of five companies matching a job simply means that any data or summary statistics for jobs with fewer than five matching companies should not be reported in the survey results. The downside is that those with only three or four companies matching may be important to those companies, but practitioners would be denied information upon which to make a decision. A practitioner would have to make compensation decisions about jobs without any information whatsoever.

Percent of a Single Statistic

While the first two requirements of the Safe Harbor guidelines may be seen as mostly inconvenient, conforming to the 25-percent dominance requirement for a job with a dominant participant can create a truly unpredictable statistical — and decision-making — situation.

Simply stated, to comply with this requirement, a single organization's dominance must be reduced. For a survey in which the data are individual salaries, the usual procedure is to bring the number of incumbents down to an acceptable level through sampling the dominant participant's data. For a survey in which the data are number of incumbents and average salary, the dominant participant's number of incumbents simply is adjusted down to an acceptable level. The statistics affected are the weighted average and, if reported, the percentiles.

It is extremely difficult to predict a priori whether the resulting statistics are lower than, the same as or higher than those that would have been reported without conforming with Safe Harbor, and by how much. A practitioner could be making compensation decisions based on a possible distortion of reality — on information believed to be correct. Sometimes these distortions can be quite significant (more than 15 percent) and the practitioner might never know it. Obviously, basing compensation program decisions on statistical distortions is not a good compensation practice.[10] The remainder of this section provides examples of what happens to statistics when conforming to the maximum dominance requirement.

Basic Statistics

Weighted Average, Unweighted Average

Technically, these terms apply when averaging averages. This frequently occurs when determining the "market pay" for a job or skill and there are averages from different companies or different surveys that need to be combined into a single number.

Weighted Average: The average of all the incumbents and mathematically equivalent to the average of the company averages weighted by the number of incumbents.

Unweighted Average: The unweighted, or simple average, of the company averages.

The weighted average is equal to the average of all the individual incumbent data. If individual incumbent data are available, it is the average of that data. If only company averages are available, it is the average of the company averages weighted by the number of incumbents. *The weighted average treats each incumbent equally.* In salary surveys, sometimes the weighted average is called the "incumbent-based average."

The unweighted average is the simple average of the company averages. The unweighted average treats each company equally. In salary survey situations, sometimes the unweighted average is called the "company-based average."

Basic Statistics (continued)

Company	Number of Incumbents	Company's Average Pay	Total Pay (Number multiplied by Average)
A	15	50,000	750,000
B	20	45,000	900,000
C	10	47,000	470,000
D	55	60,000	3,300,000
Total	100	202,000	5,420,000

Unweighted average = 202,000/4 = 50,500
Weighted average = 5,420,000/100 = 54,200

If all 100 individual salaries were available, their total would be 5.42 million with an average of 54,200. If the company with the largest weight pays high, as in this example, the weighted average will be pulled toward the high side and will be higher than the unweighted average. If the company with the largest weight pays low, the weighted average will be pulled toward the low side and will be lower than the unweighted average. If the company with the largest weight pays in the middle, the weighted average will be pulled toward the middle, and be close to the unweighted average.

Percentile

A percentile is a value that a given percentage of the data is less than or equal to. For example, the 90th percentile is a value that 90 percent of the data are less than or equal to.

To calculate a percentile of a data set, let "P" be the percent, or proportion, of the percentile, and let "N" be the number of data points. The rank or position of the percentile when the data are ordered and numbered from low to high, including numbering all the repeat values, is given by the formula $PN + (1 - P)$*. That is, the Pth percentile is the $[PN + (1 - P)]$th data value when numbered from low to high. If the $[PN + (1 - P)]$th value falls between two data points, then linear interpolation is used to calculate the value of the percentile.

*This is the formula that is used in Excel to calculate percentiles.

Source: Davis, John H. *Make Smart Decisions Using Statistics (and Excel)*, Davis Consulting, Richardson, Texas, 2003.

In the following discussions, when the term "sampling" is used, it is assumed that the resulting average of the sampled company is the same as the un-sampled average of that company. Some sampling procedures will achieve this, others will not. This is discussed later. In a survey with input data consisting only of the number of incumbents and average salary for each company, the sampling procedure is simply to change the number of incumbents; the average salary remains the same for that company.

Single Sampling of One Company

"Single sampling" means only one sampling or changing of weights is required. Another example in which iterative sampling or changing weights is required is offered later in this book. Three scenarios are shown here: Where the sampled company pays low, where it pays in the middle, and where it pays high.

In Figure 1, the dominant company (E) pays lower than most participants (see "Average Pay"). In this case, Company E originally had 43.5 percent of the data ("Incumbents"). To have no more than 25 percent, it must be sampled to have only 21 data points. Note: When sampling or changing weights, both the numerator (the number of incumbents for Company E) and the denominator (the total number of incumbents) change when calculating the resulting weight.

To comply, 58 percent of Company E's data (more than 25 percent of the total data for this job) must be discarded and, by doing so, the weighted

FIGURE 1: DOMINANT COMPANY PAYS LOW

The dominant company (E) pays lower than most participants.

No. Incumbents

	Co A	Co B	Co C	Co D	Co E	Total	
Original No Inc	15	15	15	20	50	115	
% of Total	13.0%	13.0%	13.0%	17.4%	43.5%		
1st sample	15	15	15	20	21	86	
	17.4%	17.4%	17.4%	23.3%	24.4%		
% of data discarded					58.0%	25.2%	

Average Pay

	Co A	Co B	Co C	Co D	Co E	Wtd Avg	Unwtd Avg
Original Data	9,000	8,000	7,000	6,000	5,000	6,348	7,000
1st sample	9,000	8,000	7,000	6,000	5,000	6,802	7,000
Change in weighted average						7.2%	

average moves from 6,348 to 6,802, an increase of more than 7 percent. As the weight of Company E is decreased, the weighted average for this job moves toward the unweighted average, which does not change.

In Figure 2, the dominant company (E) pays in the middle of the other participants. Here, 58 percent of Company E's data again is discarded, but because it is paying in the middle of the other participants, reducing its weight does not significantly alter the resulting weighted average. Indeed, the original weighted average is very close to the unweighted average to start.

In Figure 3, the dominant company (E) pays higher than most participants. Again, 58 percent of Company E's data is discarded, but because it pays on the high side, reducing its weights lowers the resulting weighted average by almost 6 percent. Again, the weighted average moves toward the unweighted average. Of course, the changing of weights (number of incumbents) or the average pay in any of the companies will change the specific differences in the weighted averages, but these three examples indicate the direction taken when sampling a single dominant company.

Percentiles

As some companies have a compensation policy of targeting pay toward certain percentiles, it is of interest to identify the impact of conforming to Safe Harbor guidelines. The movement of percentiles is harder to predict, but some general trends can be discussed. In general, if the dominant company pays on the low side, the sample's percentiles will be higher than the

FIGURE 2: DOMINANT COMPANY PAYS IN THE MIDDLE

The dominant company (E) pays in the middle of the other participants.

No. Incumbents

	Co A	Co B	Co C	Co D	Co E	Total	
Original No Inc	15	15	15	20	50	115	
% of total	13.0%	13.0%	13.0%	17.4%	43.5%		
1st sample	15	15	15	20	21	86	
	17.4%	17.4%	17.4%	23.3%	24.4%		
% of data discarded					58.0%	25.2%	

Average Pay

	Co A	Co B	Co C	Co D	Co E	Wtd Avg	Unwtd Avg
Original Data	5,000	6,000	9,000	8,000	7,000	7,043	7,000
1st sample	5,000	6,000	9,000	8,000	7,000	7,058	7,000
Change in weighted average						0.2%	

FIGURE 3: DOMINANT COMPANY PAYS HIGH

The dominant company (E) pays higher than most participants

No. Incumbents

	Co A	Co B	Co C	Co D	Co E	Total	
Original No Inc	15	15	15	20	50	115	
% of total	13.0%	13.0%	13.0%	17.4%	43.5%		
1st sample	15	15	15	20	21	86	
	17.4%	17.4%	17.4%	23.3%	24.4%		
% of data discarded					58.0%	25.2%	

Average Pay

	Co A	Co B	Co C	Co D	Co E	Wtd Avg	Unwtd Avg
Original Data	5,000	6,000	7,000	8,000	9,000	7,652	7,000
1st sample	5,000	6,000	7,000	8,000	9,000	7,198	7,000
Change in weighted average						-5.9%	

percentiles of the original data. However, the percentiles do not move uniformly. In Figure 1, where the dominant company paid low, P10 increased 11.2 percent, P25 increased 8.4 percent, P50 increased 12.6 percent, P75 increased 1.2 percent and P90 increased 8.0 percent. (The raw data are not shown in Figure 1.)

Again, one cannot predict a priori which will increase more than others, or even whether some will increase and others will decrease. If the dominant company pays on the high side, in general, the sample's percentiles will be lower than the percentiles of the original data. If the dominant company pays in the middle, the sample's lower percentiles will generally be lower than percentiles of the original data, the sample's higher percentiles generally will be higher than the higher percentiles of the original data, and the sample's middle percentiles will not experience significant change from the original data.

Of course, calculating percentiles is possible only when the raw data consist of individual salaries. If the raw data contain only company averages and number of incumbents, then percentiles cannot be calculated.

Single Sampling of More than One Company

In Figure 4, two dominant companies (D and E) pay higher than most of the other participants. Sometimes, multiple companies each have more than 25 percent of the raw data. In that case, each has to be sampled. Figure 5 shows

FIGURE 4: TWO DOMINANT COMPANIES PAY HIGH

Two dominant companies (D, E) pay higher than most of the other participants.

No. Incumbents

	Co A	Co B	Co C	Co D	Co E	Total	
Original No Inc	10	10	10	50	50	130	
% of total	7.7%	7.7%	7.7%	38.5%	38.5%		
1st sample	10	10	10	15	15	60	
	16.7%	16.7%	16.7%	25.0%	25.0%		
% of data discarded				70.0%	70.0%	53.8%	

Average Pay

	Co A	Co B	Co C	Co D	Co E	Wtd Avg	Unwtd Avg
Original Data	5,170	6,180	7,280	8,400	9,360	8,264	7,278
1st sample	5,170	6,180	7,280	8,400	9,360	7,545	7,278
Change in weighted average						-8.7%	

two companies, each with 38.5 percent of the data. Seventy percent of each of their data must be discarded to bring the companies into Safe Harbor compliance. In this example, both companies D and E are high payers, and the weighted average decreases by almost 9 percent. More than half of the entire raw data set has been discarded.

Iterative Sampling

In Figure 5, dominant companies D and E pay higher than most of the other participants. Sometimes, when one company's weight is brought down to 25 percent, another company's weight jumps above 25 percent, and then it, too, has to be sampled. In frequent cases, when the second company's weight is brought down, the first company pops up again, and so on. In Figure 6, companies D and E seesaw with sampling in the quest for each to achieve no more than a 25-percent weight. Four iterations are required. More than 60 percent of the raw data have been discarded, and the weighted average is decreased by more than 11 percent.

In Figure 6, dominant companies D and E pay lower than most of the other participants. Here, the change in weighted average is more than 16 percent, which is quite large.

This discussion demonstrates that sampling or changing weights to lower dominance to conform to Safe Harbor can distort both the weighted average and the percentiles for a given job. Thus, results based on compliance with Safe Harbor Guidelines can give a distorted and misleading view. Without

FIGURE 5: TWO DOMINANT COMPANIES PAY HIGH, ITERATIVE SAMPLING

Two dominant companies (D, E) pay higher than most of the other participants.

No. Incumbents

	Co A	Co B	Co C	Co D	Co E	Total	
Original No Inc	10	10	10	40	90	160	
% of total	6.3%	6.3%	6.3%	25.0%	56.3%		
1st sample	10	10	10	40	23	93	
	10.8%	10.8%	10.8%	43.0%	24.7%		
2nd sample	10	10	10	17	23	70	
	14.3%	14.3%	14.3%	24.3%	32.9%		
3rd sample	10	10	10	17	15	62	
	16.1%	16.1%	16.1%	27.4%	24.2%		
4th sample	10	10	10	15	15	60	
	16.7%	16.7%	16.7%	25.0%	25.0%		
% of data discarded				62.5%	83.3%	62.5%	

Average Pay

	Co A	Co B	Co C	Co D	Co E	Wtd Avg	Unwtd Avg
Original Data	5,346	6,365	7,571	8,820	9,734	8,886	7,567
1st sample	5,346	6,365	7,571	8,820	9,734	8,274	7,567
2nd sample	5,346	6,365	7,571	8,820	9,734	8,095	7,567
3rd sample	5,346	6,365	7,571	8,820	9,734	7,884	7,567
4th sample	5,346	6,365	7,571	8,820	9,734	7,852	7,567
Change in weighted average						-11.6%	

access to the raw data, it is virtually impossible to predict the direction or degree of distortion. The only observable trend is that the weighted average of the sampled data tends to move toward the unweighted average. (See "Which Measure to Use?")

FIGURE 6: TWO DOMINANT COMPANIES PAY LOW, ITERATIVE SAMPLING

Two dominant companies (D, E) pay lower than most of the other participants.

No. Incumbents

	Co A	Co B	Co C	Co D	Co E	Total
Original No Inc	10	10	10	40	90	160
% of total	6.3%	6.3%	6.3%	25.0%	56.3%	
1st sample	10	10	10	40	23	93
	10.8%	10.8%	10.8%	43.0%	24.7%	
2nd sample	10	10	10	17	23	70
	14.3%	14.3%	14.3%	24.3%	32.9%	
3rd sample	10	10	10	17	15	62
	16.1%	16.1%	16.1%	27.4%	24.2%	
4th sample	10	10	10	15	15	60
	16.7%	16.7%	16.7%	25.0%	25.0%	
% of data discarded				62.5%	83.3%	62.5%

Average Pay

	Co A	Co B	Co C	Co D	Co E	Wtd Avg	Unwtd Avg
Original Data	9,000	8,000	7,000	6,000	5,000	5,813	7,000
1st sample	9,000	8,000	7,000	6,000	5,000	6,398	7,000
2nd sample	9,000	8,000	7,000	6,000	5,000	6,529	7,000
3rd sample	9,000	8,000	7,000	6,000	5,000	6,726	7,000
4th sample	9,000	8,000	7,000	6,000	5,000	6,750	7,000
Change in weighted average						16.1%	

Which Measure to Use?

The answer is, "It depends." The most common market reference points chosen against which to posture a compensation program are the weighted average, the unweighted average and the median. Following are comments that give a perspective on these three. Comments regarding choosing various percentiles are not given here.

Weighted Average: One argument for using the weighted average is that it reflects equally the number of incumbents in the survey, which, if the companies participating truly are representative of the chosen market, reflects the market value of the job or skill. The number of incumbents represents the number of potential openings for that job or skill.

In the extreme, if there were only two companies in the market — one with 10 incumbents and one with 1,000 incumbents — then the one with the 1,000 is determining the market, and the weighted average would be the measure to use. In other words, if there is a dominant company, then that *is* the market. If all the chosen competitors are participants in the survey, then the weighted average would make sense. And, even if they were not all in the survey, *if the survey is representative of the chosen market, and it is desired to target pay levels at the average pay of the market incumbents, then choose the weighted average.*

Unweighted Average: One argument for using the unweighted average is that, due to the sampling process of getting companies to participate in the survey, there may be a company with a large number of incumbents that is not in the survey, and may be unknowingly on the high or low side of the data.

Expanding on the aforementioned example, suppose there were a third party with 1,000 incumbents that was in the market, but their data are not available, so it cannot be determined whether they are a low, middle or high payer. One may consider hedging one's bet in giving all the weight to the 1,000-incumbent company for which data is available.

In this case, giving equal weight to each company would make sense to determine the "typical" or "representative" value for that job or skill. In other words, *if you are not sure of the survey representativeness for the chosen competition, then choose the unweighted average.*

Combination Average: Some companies use a combination average,

Which Measure to Use? (continued)

which is the average of the weighted average and the unweighted average. This gives equal weight to both the number of incumbents and the number of companies.

Median: One argument for using the median is that it is not affected by extremely high or low values. By its very nature of using all the information, the weighted average is influenced by both the companies with the highest number of incumbents and the companies that pay very high or very low. Sometimes these balance out, but *if you want to avoid the influence of outliers, or just want to reference the middle of the market pay, then choose the median.*

Source: Davis, John H. *Make Smart Decisions Using Statistics (and Excel)*, Davis Consulting, Richardson, Texas, 2003.

One factor that makes any prediction difficult is the varied distribution of salary survey data. If there were a consistent distribution, one might assume that the dominant participant's data were close to the mode, then make some generalized predictions based on that. However, survey distributions are varied.[11]

The next page shows examples of the smoothed distribution of data for 10 jobs from an actual survey. As shown, the distributions can be positively skewed, negatively skewed, bell-shaped, uniform, bimodal and trimodal. As an aside, it would be an exceedingly rare occurrence for a job to have its data normally distributed.

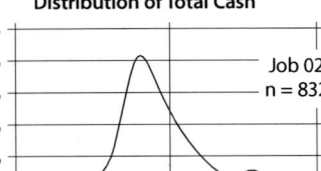
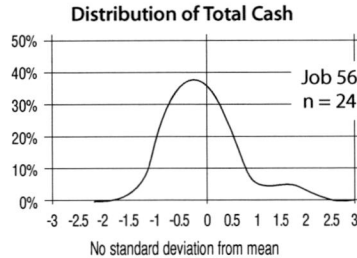
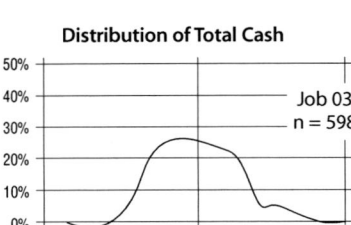
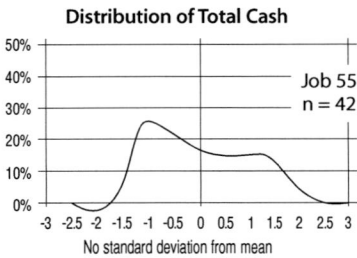
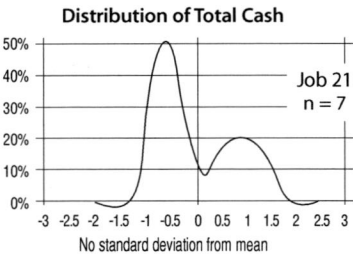
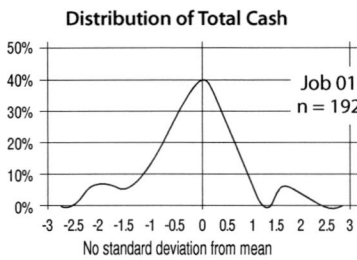
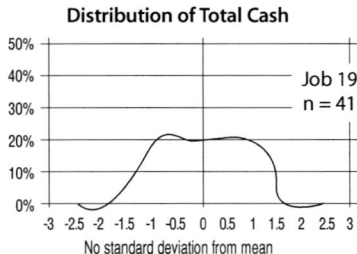
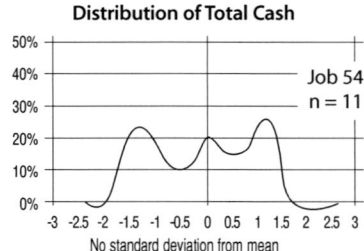
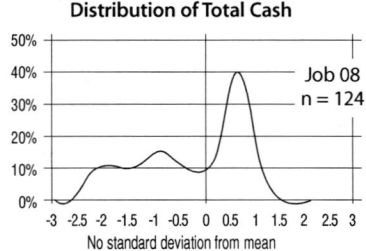
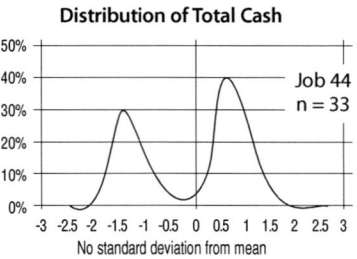

Year-to-Year Trends

Compensation practitioners (and especially their company executives) often wonder, "What happened in the market last year?" To answer this, they look at year-to-year trend data. However, with or without Safe Harbor Guidelines, trends need to be interpreted with caution, as there is inherent variability in the pay trend for a given job from one year to the next. Reasons for this variability include:

- Changes in the companies matching
- Changes in the number of incumbents matched for a given company
- Changes in the incumbents themselves (new incumbents in this year, but not in last year, and old incumbents in last year, but not in this year)
- Changes in pay policies that affect pay raises, special one-time salary adjustments, unusual budget constraints, etc.

To the degree that these factors are known or not present is the degree to which one can rely on trend data. To address this, a few sophisticated surveys have been able to collect identifiers for individual incumbents and are able to report out three trends for each job:

- *Traditional trend or "total companies" trend.* This compares all companies matching with all their matched incumbents from the previous year to all companies matching with all their matched incumbents for this year.
- *Constant companies trend.* This compares only those companies matching the job both years with whatever incumbents they had for each year.
- *Constant incumbent or constant employee trend.* This compares only those incumbents matching the job both years, using the incumbent identifiers as a mechanism.

Experience with these three types of survey analysis reveals that the three trend numbers almost always are different from each other. Typically, participants favor the constant employee comparison because they believe it gives them the truest measure of what is happening in the market for those jobs.

But sampling to address dominance (as required by the Safe Harbor Guidelines) could seriously undermine the ability to make such constant employee comparisons on the sampled data, as it is most probable that some of the constant employees would be sampled one year and not the next.

Furthermore, sampling to address dominance only adds additional variability to the aforementioned factors and makes the use of traditional trend data even more tenuous. Taking the data from Figures 4, 5 and 6, it is clear in Figure 7 that the "total companies" trends based on weighted averages of the original data differ from those based on the sampled data. If Company E is increasingly dominant for this job, then the market in reality is going to be at the level Company E pays. The trends of weighted averages taking its dominance into account are higher and more realistic than those shown for the sampled data. Note that the Safe Harbor trends tend to be closer to the trends of the unweighted averages, as the Safe Harbor weighted averages tend toward the unweighted averages.

Summary of Statistical Implications

While complying with the Safe Harbor three-month requirement renders evergreen surveys less useful, and complying with the five-company minimum can entirely eliminate data for jobs with only three or four matching companies, complying with the 25-percent dominance rule can cause significant statistical variability.

Complying with the 25-percent dominance rule by changing weights or sampling the raw data can result in unpredictable and inconsistent weighted averages and percentiles. For a given job, the distribution is unknown, the degree of required sampling is unpredictable and the pay levels of dominant participants are unknown.

Different companies often dominate different jobs within a given survey for a given year. Different companies often dominate different jobs from one

FIGURE 7: TRENDS FROM ONE YEAR TO THE NEXT

Reality Trends

	No Inc	% Change	Wtd Avg	% Change	Unwtd Avg	% Change
Year 1 (Fig. 3)	115		7,652		7,000	
Year 2 (Fig. 4)	130	13.0%	8,264	8.0%	7,278	4.0%
Year 3 (Fig. 5)	160	23.1%	8,886	7.5%	7,567	4.0%

Safe Harbor Trends

	No Inc	% Change	Wtd Avg	% Change
Year 1 (Fig. 3)	86		7,198	
Year 2 (Fig. 4)	60	-30.2%	7,545	4.8%
Year 3 (Fig. 5)	60	0.0%	7,852	4.1%

year to the next. Sampling or changing weights to conform to Safe Harbor Guidelines can result in a distorted and misleading view of what really is happening in the market.

COMPENSATION PRACTITIONERS AND SALARY SURVEY PRACTICES

COMPENSATION PRACTITIONERS AND SALARY SURVEY PRACTICES

When considering policy or practice changes, companies often want to know what others are doing in the same area. To inform compensation practitioners and their organizations, a questionnaire was electronically sent in September 2002 to a random, stratified sample of the WorldatWork membership to identify trends in salary survey practices. The results were tabulated and sent to participants in October 2002.[12]

As mentioned in the Executive Summary, the survey found that more than half of the organizations queried have no guidelines — either formal or informal — regarding their participation in, or use of, salary surveys. More than one-third of companies require a minimum number of matches for a job from survey providers, with slightly less requiring a maximum allowable dominance for a job. Virtually all organizations indicated they had participated in third-party surveys (conducted by consulting firms, etc.) during the previous 12 months, and more than 60 percent also participated in non-third party surveys (i.e., surveys conducted by a survey participant, not a consulting firm).

A total of 564 responses was received from U.S. members, each representing a different organization. An additional 44 responses were received from Canadian members; however, their data are not included in this report, as this article explores the impact of U.S. antitrust law on salary surveys. All further discussion in this report pertains to U.S. companies only.[13] The distribution size of respondent organizations is shown in Figure 8.

With one exception, the responses did not vary significantly by organization size. Hence, it is believed that the data and trends are representative of the WorldatWork membership. To the degree that WorldatWork members are representative of organizations in general, these trends will apply. The survey on salary survey practices by compensation practitioners focused on two primary issues:

- Salary surveys conducted by consulting firms or other third parties
- Salary surveys not conducted by consulting firms or other third parties, meaning these surveys were conducted by the company itself or by one of the participants in the survey.

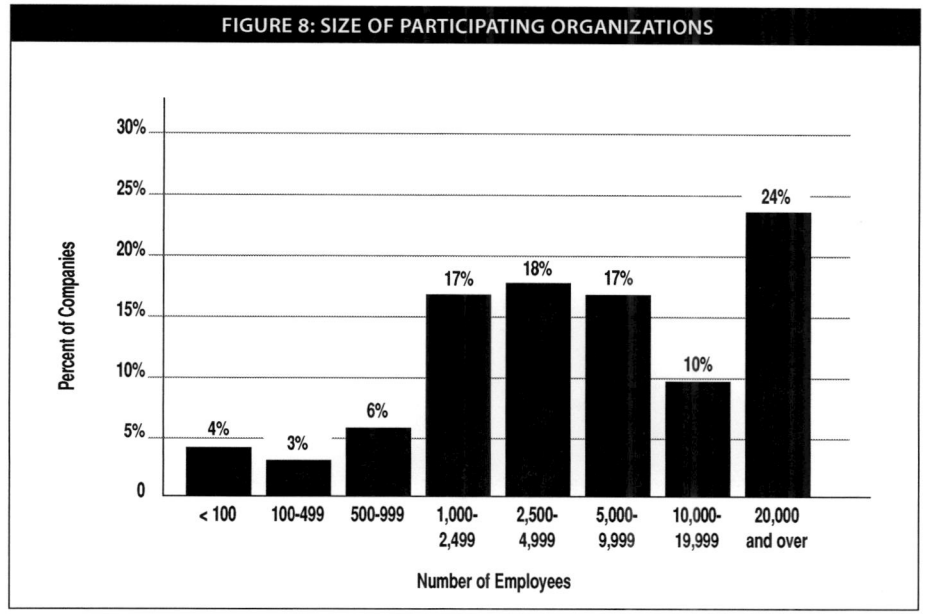

Salary Surveys Conducted by Third Parties

Figure 9 shows the number of salary surveys that respondents indicated participating in during the previous 12 months. On the whole, most organizations participate in fewer than 10 salary surveys per year. This is one of the areas in which company size made a difference; smaller firms tended to participate in just a few surveys. Of the companies with less than 1,000 employees, 74 percent reported participating in just one to five surveys, and only 4 percent reported participating in more than 15. Respondents were asked about their practices regarding consulting firm/third-party surveys in two areas:

- Participating in a survey in the first place
- Using the survey results.

A major thrust of the Safe Harbor Guidelines focuses on the minimum number of companies matching a job and the maximum dominance of a company for a job. Therefore, many of the questions were directed toward those areas. Figure 10 summarizes the results of this part of the survey. For the most part, there are no major differences between the requirements to participate in a survey and the requirements to use survey results.

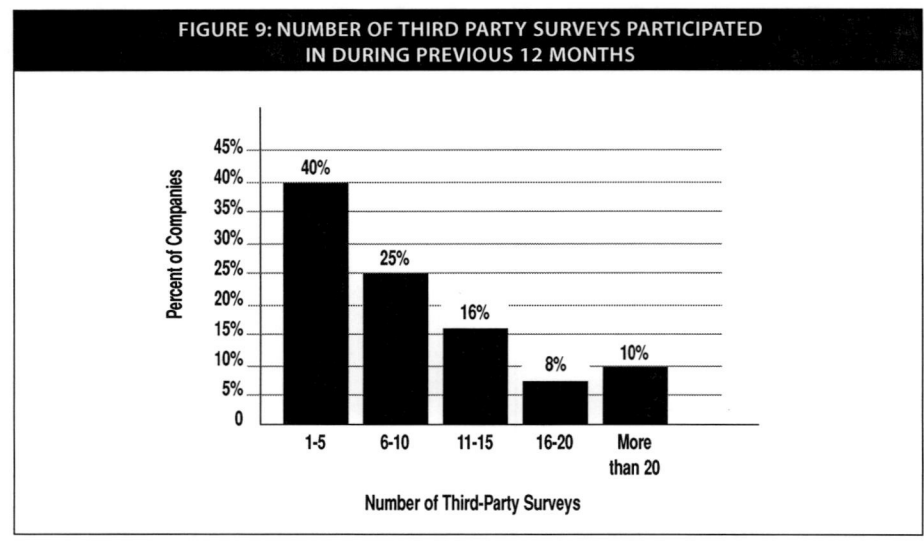

FIGURE 9: NUMBER OF THIRD PARTY SURVEYS PARTICIPATED IN DURING PREVIOUS 12 MONTHS

Elaboration on Minimum Number of Matches

With regard to gaining assurance from the surveyor *before participation* that there will be a minimum number of companies matching a reported job, the two most predominant reasons given under the "It depends" response were the reputation and credibility of the survey and survey provider, and who the participating companies were.

Regarding whether to have a minimum number of companies matching any given job *when using the data*, the two most predominant and related reasons given under the "It depends" response were the job (i.e., its uniqueness, how hard it is to fill) and the difficulty of finding data.

Also, three respondents explained what they do when they have to use sparse data:

- "I … will comment on the questionable validity."
- "…We … would not weight the information heavily in our compensation decision."
- "We also will point out to management that the data are flawed."

Certainly it is a good practice to give an assessment of the validity of and your comfort with the survey data, as these three suggest.

Some respondents elaborated on the term "statistical validity" as it relates to the rationale requiring a minimum number of matches for a job. The theme

	To participate in a survey Rules or guidelines for participation in surveys	To use survey results Rules or guidelines for using survey results
Formal/written	3%	7%
Informal/unwritten	36%	40%
None	59%	52%
	Seek assurance from surveyor there will be a minimum number of matches for each job reported, before participating	Require a minimum number of matches for any given job in order to use the results for that job
Yes, always	38%	48%
No	36%	29%
It depends	15%	23%
Of those that said YES, the minimum number of matches is		
3	10%	19%
5	49%	42%
10 or more	34%	27%
Other (2,4,6,7,8,9)	7%	12%
Of those that said YES, the rationale is (multiple responses)		
Statistical validity	80%	88%
Compensation policy	16%	18%
Legal reasons	31%	13%
Always done it that way	8%	10%
Other	20%	10%
	Seek assurance from surveyor that a single company will not dominate the data for each job reported, before participating	Require that a single company will not dominate the data for any given job in order to use the results for that job
Yes, always	23%	39%
No	68%	49%
It depends	10%	12%
Of those that said YES, the maximum dominance of a single company is		
25%	25%	20%
30%	24%	19%
35%	19%	26%
Other %	14%	18%
Other non-% response	19%	18%
Of those that said YES, the rationale is (multiple responses)		
Statistical validity	87%	87%
Compensation policy	18%	16%
Legal reasons	13%	9%
Always done it that way	6%	7%
Other	12%	7%

FIGURE 10: RESPONSES CONCERNING GUIDELINES, MATCHES AND DOMINANCE

of this elaboration is that having a minimum number of matches gives confidence that there are sufficient data points to adequately describe what the market among the survey participants really is paying. A small number of data points or companies may not identify a trend, where a large number would raise the confidence that any trend that exists has been captured with the data. (See "Statistical Validity.") Regarding the rationale requiring a minimum number of matches for a job, half of the respondents checking "other" cited confidentiality as the reason.

Elaboration on Maximum Domination of a Company

There were not themes in the "It depends" responses regarding whether to seek assurances from the surveyor before participation that no one company would dominate any given job in the reported results. Most (87 percent) of the respondents who did have maximum dominance requirements indicated statistical validity as the rationale for that requirement.

There were no themes in the "Other" response regarding the rationale for requiring a maximum dominance. However, three respondents responded that no one company determines the market.

Salary Surveys Not Conducted by Consultants or Other Third Parties

Sixty-one percent of the respondents participated in salary surveys conducted either by themselves or another non-consulting firm that participated in the survey. These surveys will be referred to as "non-third-party surveys."

The following discussion pertains only to those respondents who participate in non-third-party surveys. The percentages in the figures refer to the percent of respondents that gave a particular response. Figure 11 shows the number of these types of surveys in which respondents have participated; the majority participated in five or fewer.

Unlike third-party surveys, there was no relation between company size and the number of non-third-party surveys. Just 2 percent of the respondents had formal or written guidelines for non-third-party surveys. (See Figure 12.) This is very similar to the responses about guidelines for third-party surveys.

Data exchanges occur in a variety of ways. As shown in Figure 13 (multiple responses allowed), the predominant method is electronic, such as e-mail or e-mail attachments. Figure 14 indicates the prevalence of the types and sizes of non-third-party surveys. Some companies that marked "None" for one type of

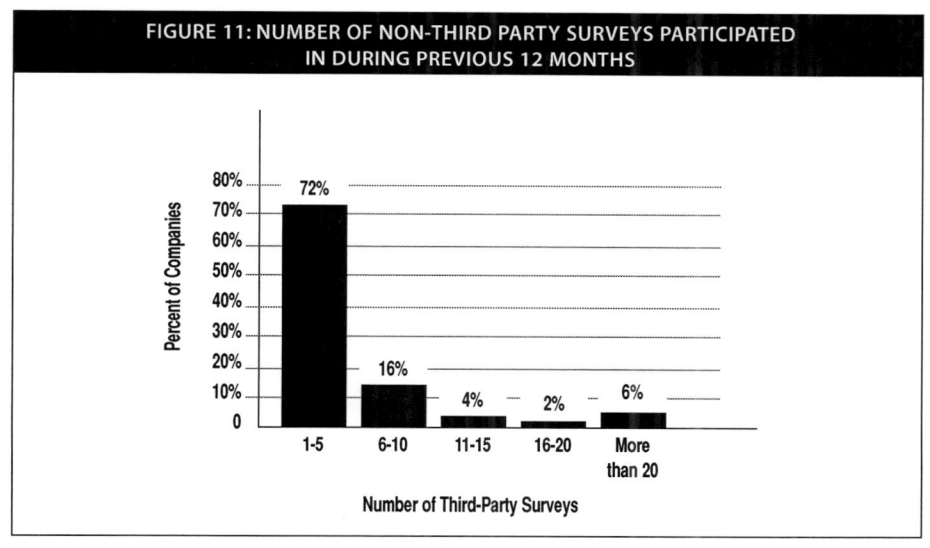

FIGURE 12: FORMAL OR WRITTEN GUIDELINES FOR NON-THIRD PARTY SURVEYS

Formal or written guidelines	2%
Informal or unwritten guidelines	41%
No guidelines or rules	56%

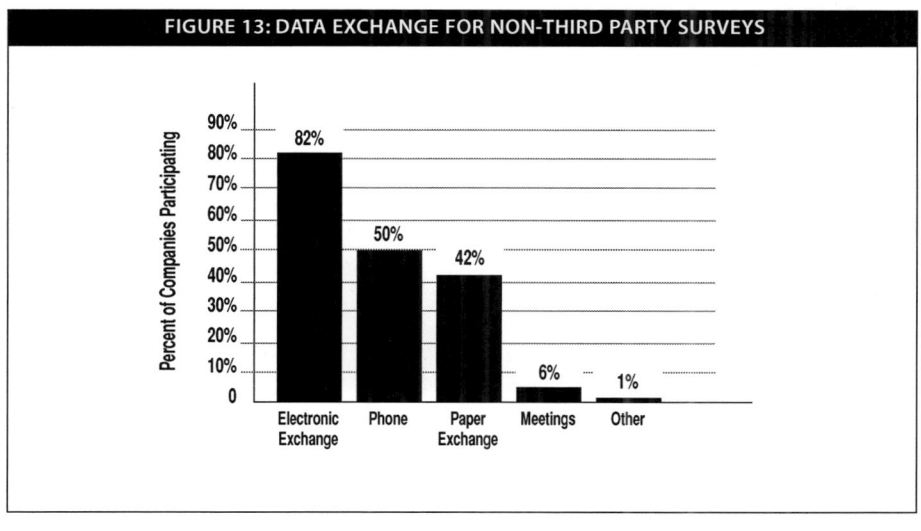

SALARY SURVEYS AND ANTITRUST | 43

survey participated in the other type of survey. Many participated in both. Ad hoc surveys tended to have fewer jobs, while annual surveys had more.

FIGURE 14: PREVALENCE OF TYPES AND SIZES OF NON-THIRD PARTY SURVEYS

The table below indicates the prevalence of the types and sizes of non-third-party surveys.

	One-time, ad hoc surveys	Annual, ongoing surveys
Number of surveys		
None	14%	41%
1 - 5	66%	51%
6 - 10	11%	4%
More than 10	8%	4%
Average number of jobs in survey		
1 - 5	67%	18%
6 - 10	20%	18%
11 - 15	6%	13%
16 - 20	3%	12%
More than 20	4%	39%

Safe Harbor Guidelines

The good news is, only 10 percent of respondents to the entire survey never had heard of the Safe Harbor Guidelines. The bad news is, only 16 percent were "very familiar" with them. (See Figure 15.) It is hoped that this study will expand awareness and familiarity.

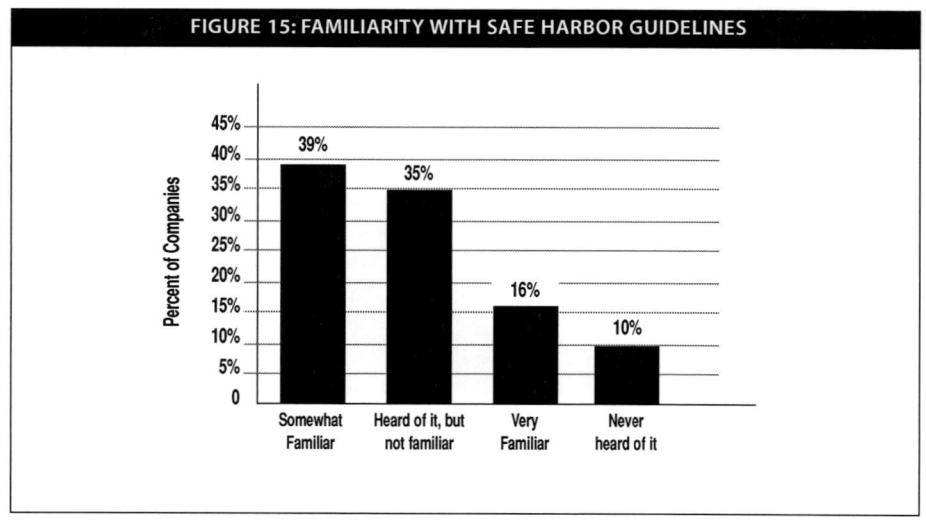

FIGURE 15: FAMILIARITY WITH SAFE HARBOR GUIDELINES

Statistical Validity

What does it mean for a reported statistic for a matched job, such as the weighted average or a percentile, to have statistical validity? If the statistic is to be used for decision-making, there first must be content validity in the data from which the statistic is calculated.

Content Validity

The numbers have to be measured on the same characteristic and entities relevant to what is being studied:

- Don't mix base pay and number of employees supervised. These are different characteristics of the entities being measured.
- Don't mix the pay for an entry-level job with the pay for a journey-level job. This is the same characteristic, but for two different types of entities.

Generally, ensuring the same characteristic is measured is not an issue for salary surveys. Compensation practitioners and survey providers do not mix measurements such as salary, bonus, total cash or stock options. Rather, the issue for salary surveys concerns the relevancy of the entity being measured and, in particular, the homogeneity of the entity being measured. The two main salary survey factors here are the relevancy of the companies matching the job and the job matches themselves. With regard to the companies matching the job, the key point is that they are representative of the chosen market reference. Criteria typically used to define competition include companies that:

- Do what you do
- Have jobs like yours
- Are your size
- Are in the same locations
- Hire employees from you
- Lose employees to you.

Sometimes different criteria are used for different jobs. The point is that the companies in the survey should be representative of the chosen competition.

Job matching is the most important component of a salary survey —

Statistical Validity (continued)

"apples to apples" are matched and you can ensure that market data match the jobs you are interested in. In short, it ensures the homogeneity of what is being measured. Choosing relevant companies for compensation program comparison purposes and various job matching processes are discussed in detail by Davis and Koechel[14] and will not be repeated here.

Statistical Validity

A statistic is valid if it is both unbiased and precise. Trochim[15] illustrates this with a metaphor, using the terms "valid" and "reliable" for "unbiased" and "precise," respectively.

We often think of reliability and validity as separate ideas, but in fact, they're related to each other. Here, I want to show you two ways you can think about their relationship.

One of my favorite metaphors for the relationship between reliability and validity is that of the target. Think of the center of the target as the concept that you are trying to measure. Imagine that for each person you are measuring, you are taking a shot at the target. If you measure the concept perfectly for a person, you are hitting the center of the target. If you don't, you are missing the center. The more you are off for that person, the further you are from the center. Figure 16 shows four possible solutions. In the first, you are hitting the target consistently, but you are missing the center of the target. That is, you are consistently and systematically measuring the wrong value for all respondents. This measure is reliable, but not valid (that is, it's consistent but wrong). The second

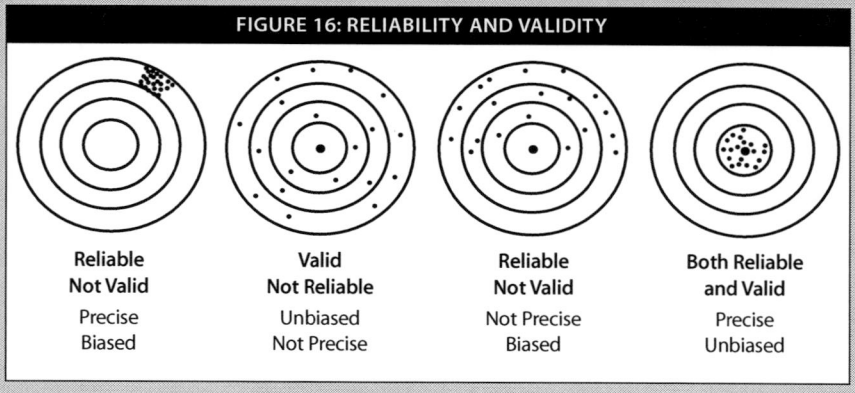

FIGURE 16: RELIABILITY AND VALIDITY

Reliable Not Valid	Valid Not Reliable	Reliable Not Valid	Both Reliable and Valid
Precise Biased	Unbiased Not Precise	Not Precise Biased	Precise Unbiased

Statistical Validity (continued)

shows hits that are randomly spread across the target. You seldom hit the center of the target, but on average, you are getting the right answer for the group (but not very well for individuals). In this case, you get a valid group estimate, but you are inconsistent. Here, you clearly can see that reliability is directly related to the variability of your measure. The third scenario shows a case where your hits are spread across the target and you are consistently missing the center. Your measure in this case is neither reliable nor valid. Finally, we see the "Robin Hood" scenario — you consistently hit the center of the target. Your measure is both reliable and valid.

For salary surveys, the more important of these two is that the statistic should be unbiased. Whether data are tight (precise) or loose (spread out), the calculated average or percentile should be "on the money" and not inadvertently high or low. For many jobs there is a sense of the reasonability of the precision — or lack thereof. If the data are spread out more than expected, they should be examined to check for content validity and data errors. If those check out, then the data are just spread out for that job and there is high variability. A related issue is the number of data points from which the statistic is calculated. Naturally, there is a desire to have as many as possible, but usually we have to work with what we've got. It's a judgment call as to how many companies or incumbents are needed to give a comfort level that there are sufficient data to identify the pay levels for a job.

In summary, factors that influence the validity of salary survey statistics include:

- Content validity of what is being measured
  - Representativeness of the chosen market of the companies matching
  - Sound job matches
- Statistical validity of the measurement
  - Unbiased
  - Precise
  - Number of data points from which the statistic is calculated.

SALARY SURVEY PRACTICES AMONG CONSULTING FIRMS

SALARY SURVEY PRACTICES AMONG CONSULTING FIRMS

Besides knowing the survey practices of survey participants, organizations also want to know the practices of consulting firms that conduct surveys. This study obtained information from 12 consulting firms to identify the degree to which the Safe Harbor rules affect or could affect the salary surveys they conduct. The surveyed firms ranged from major consulting firms that provide a full spectrum of HR consulting services to boutique firms that only conduct surveys. The study found that consulting firms vary in their approach to the Safe Harbor requirements. Recall the three statistical areas that can be affected by Safe Harbor:

- Data less than three months old may not be used.
- If there are insufficient companies matching a job, the results are simply not reported.
- If there is dominance of the data by a company, the three statistics affected are:
  - Weighted average
  - Percentiles
  - Number of incumbents underlying the weighted average and percentiles.

The unweighted average would not be affected.

There were a variety of business models and subsequent ways the firms gathered and provided data, which made the sought-after information to the initial inquiry more complex.

Number of Surveys Conducted

The answer to "How many surveys do you conduct in a year?" is not straightforward in the usual context of what is meant by the term "survey." Three examples will illustrate.

- There used to be separate annual surveys of identical jobs in six locations. Then they were consolidated into a national survey with six geographic breakouts. Is this now one survey, or is it still six?

- The "survey" consists of a database from which participants select companies and jobs for their particular cuts, subject to certain rules. Is this one survey or several thousand?
- The survey is an industry survey with five sections: hourly, office and clerical, professional and managerial, sales and executive. Some sections collect and report different types of data. Is this one survey or five?

With this as a perspective, the number of surveys conducted ranged from a reported one with various sections, to a 40-plus in a national database with thousands of participants who get their custom reports via the firm's Web site.

One large firm reported conducting 25 from a local office, but it was unknown how many were conducted from other offices. If the other offices were similar, the number of separate surveys would be in the hundreds. This was in addition to a rolling database they maintained for their national survey information.

Number of Jobs Surveyed

The number of jobs surveyed by any given firm ranged from 1,000 to 4,000. The round numbers are all estimates by the respondents. Even one survey with different sections had around 1,000 jobs.

Minimum Number of Companies Matching a Job to Report Results

A slight majority said the minimum number of companies required to match a job to report the results is three. The remainder said five. However, several respondents said it depended on the survey. Some surveys required as many as 10 minimum matching companies to report. Two respondents with a requirement of three matching companies also required a minimum of five incumbents among those three. Two of the firms that required three companies reported additional requirements on the required minimum number of incumbents to report percentiles. (See Figure 17.)

For companies with databases allowing participants to get their own cuts via the Internet, there are a minimum number of companies required for a cut, ranging from three to eight, with five being most common. The required minimum number of companies matching a particular job

FIGURE 17: MINIMUM NUMBER OF INCUMBENTS TO REPORT PERCENTILES

Percentile	Firm 1	Firm 2
P10	10	10
P25	6	5
P50	4	3
P75	6	5
P90	10	10

typically is programmed into the software generating the report. Some surveys have higher requirements on the minimum number of companies for a cut.

Maximum Dominance Allowed for a Company to Report the Results

Half the respondents had no internal policies allowing a maximum dominance for a job before reporting the results. Among these, one reported that it varied by survey and situation. Another had some surveys that allowed 25 percent to 35 percent dominance.

About one-third of respondents had a policy of 25 percent, of which one had more stringent requirements for demographic breakouts. One firm had a policy of allowing one-third dominance (33.3 percent).

Among those with policy requirements, sometimes the dominance percentage also is required for data cuts, and sometimes it isn't, in which case they adjust for dominance for the overall survey results, but do not readjust for cuts. Some surveys themselves, via the sponsor or steering committee, impose dominance requirements for cuts in addition to imposing them for the overall survey results.

Adjusting for Dominance

Several methods for addressing dominance were reported. Mostly, firms collected pay data on individual incumbents. Methods included:

- Stratified sampling
- Serial sampling
- Proprietary algorithm to reduce the weights for both the weighted average and the percentiles.

One firm reported that, if the dominant company is centered in the data, they leave it alone. If it skews the data, they reduce its dominance by serial sampling. Another firm, for surveys collecting just the number of incumbents and average from each company for a matched job, simply adjusts the weight of the dominant company to reduce it to a desired weight.

Typically, dominance is not an issue, as many large surveys have such a large number of companies matching the jobs. Dominance tends to be more of an issue with small industry surveys, and with highly specialized jobs in a survey in which only a few companies are able to match.

For some surveys among public sector participants, dominance and confidentiality are not issues, as the pay of individual employees is public information (obtainable).

Adjusting for Dominance

Surveys with Starting Data of Number of Incumbents and Average Pay

For a survey with starting data of just number of incumbents and average pay for each company, adjusting for dominance is straightforward.

Let

N_{orig} = the original number of incumbents for the dominant company

N_{adj} = the adjusted number of incumbents for the dominant company

N_{other} = the number of incumbents of the remaining participants

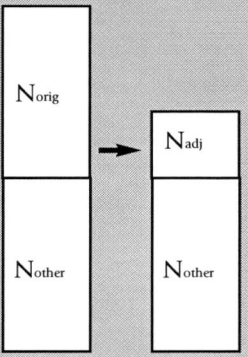

We want — $N_{adj}/(N_{adj} + N_{other}) = 0.25$ (25 percent)

Using algebra to solve for N_{adj} we get — $N_{adj} = N_{other}/3$

Example

In the survey below, Company F has $50/125 = 40$ percent of the data. We want to adjust its dominance to 25 percent. Using the above formula

$$N_{other} = 125 - 50 = 75$$

$$N_{adj} = 75 / 3 = 25$$

Adjusting for Dominance (continued)

With the adjusted number of incumbents, Company F now has 25/100 = 25 percent of the data.

Company	Original No. Inc.	Average Pay	Total Pay	Adjusted No. Inc.	Average Pay	Total Pay
A	15	48,000	720,000	15	48,000	720,000
B	12	52,000	624,000	12	52,000	624,000
C	15	50,000	750,000	15	50,000	750,000
D	20	45,000	900,000	20	45,000	900,000
E	13	47,000	611,000	13	47,000	611,000
F	50	60,000	3,000,000	25	60,000	1,500,000
Total	125		6,605,000	100		5,105,000
Wtd Avg		52,840			51,050	

Of course, this example is for a single adjustment. As previously illustrated, iterative adjustments may be necessary. Those adjustments may be made by applying the formula above. If the desired dominance is more than 25 percent, a different formula would result.

Surveys with Starting Data of Individual Incumbent Salaries

There are several ways to address dominance in surveys of this type, such as sampling the dominant company to reduce its number of data points.

Serial Sampling

With this method, the data for the dominant company is first sorted by salary. Then, every so many data points are selected, depending on the amount of adjustment needed. In "Adjusting for Dominance," where Company F originally had 50 incumbents and you wanted the sample to contain 25, you first would sort the company's salaries, then take every other one. This is a 50-percent sample. Or, suppose you had a situation in which you need a 40-percent (or two-fifths) sample. In this case, one method of serial sampling would be to first sort, then take two, skip three, take two, skip three, and so on. You would be taking two-fifths of the data for the sample. There are different techniques to conduct serial sampling, but this gives the general idea.

The advantage of serial sampling is that the sample has the same, or almost the same, distribution as the original data for the company. For example, if the original data for Company F were skewed positively, the sample data for Company F also would be skewed positively.

Adjusting for Dominance (continued)

Stratified Sampling

For a survey with different categories of data, such as geographic location or industry, to preserve information about the dominant company among the categories and ensure that cuts by these categories contain data from the sampled company, stratified sampling is conducted. The data for the dominant company first is sorted by category (stratum) and within each category, sorted by salary. Then the data are sampled within each category according to the degree needed.

Random Sampling

None of the firms reported random sampling, but it is mentioned here nonetheless. In the context of salary surveys and Safe Harbor, random sampling would not be appropriate for reducing dominance. Random sampling is used when the parameters of the population being sampled are unknown. But here, the population is known — namely the data from the dominant company. You want to represent it as best as possible with your sample, which is what serial sampling and stratified sampling do. With random sampling, due to its very nature, all the high salaries or all the low salaries may, by chance, be sampled. But that is not what is wanted. Consistency and representativeness are the desired qualities of the sample.

Other

One firm mentioned a proprietary algorithm that preserved the original data but just adjusted weights to calculate non-dominant weighted averages and percentiles. The respondent mentioned it had been tested and verified with many jobs. The firm did not disclose the standard for verification.

Impact of Complying with Safe Harbor

The impact of complying with Safe Harbor varies widely among individual surveys.

Minimum Number of Companies

For startup surveys within an industry group, especially where there are specialized jobs, the impact can be severe. For example, in one annual specialized industry survey, more than 40 percent of the jobs had only three or four companies matching them. Firms estimated the proportion of jobs that have only three or four companies matching (regardless of whether they report them) between 3 percent and 7 percent.

Dominance

As mentioned, dominance tends to be more of an issue for smaller surveys, especially surveys conducted for industry groups in which there are a smaller number of participants and/or where there are highly specialized jobs. For example, in three industry surveys, 46 percent, 75 percent and 85 percent, respectively, of the jobs had at least one company submit more than 25 percent of the data. Different companies dominated different jobs.

The estimates given by firms of the proportion of jobs that had a company submit more than 25 percent of the data (regardless of whether they adjusted for dominance) ranged between zero and 40 percent of the jobs, with the predominant estimate being 10 percent.

Issues

Respondents raised several issues.

- Evergreen surveys collect and submit data to a database year-round. Participants can request special cuts at any time. Some data in the database are current — say a week or two old. This does not comply with the Safe Harbor requirement that data be at least three months old.

- "If one submits a salary to a firm, database or another requesting company, it typically is the current salary of the incumbent. How do they know whether the salary level was granted one week or eight months ago? Is it still effective as the date I gave it?"

- If sharing planned actions raises antitrust concerns, how does that impact surveys that gather and report projected salary increase budgets?

In summary, consulting firms vary in their approach to addressing the number of matching companies and dominance. For many large surveys, neither of these is an issue.

THE VIEWS OF ATTORNEYS

THE VIEWS OF ATTORNEYS

Discussions with four attorneys revealed a variety of views regarding safe harbor guidelines, but all tended toward prudence. The following discussion contains the thoughts and opinions of the attorneys interviewed. All of the attorneys requested confidentiality for themselves and their organizations.

Attorney No. 1

This attorney advised his compensation department to play it safe by complying with the spirit and letter of the Safe Harbor guidelines. He also said that having a third party collect the salary data, in his mind, added objectivity and accuracy to the process. His overall counsel to his organization was to err on the side of caution.

Attorney No. 2

Similar to Attorney No. 1, this attorney said that, through their issuance of the Safe Harbor guidelines, the DOJ and FTC have indicated that they would not prosecute organizations that operated within the parameters. With these guidelines, she opined, it is foolhardy to operate outside for the possibility of obtaining slightly better data. Her point was: Why run the risk? Because damages are trebled immediately, the risk-to-reward ratio was greatly out of balance on the side of risk.

Attorney No. 3

This attorney took a slightly more relaxed position. He indicated that it is better to operate within the guidelines, but by no means is it absolutely necessary. He added that there are gray areas, and it is possible to conduct a pro-competitive salary survey outside of Safe Harbor. His recommendation would be to get legal advice for each situation, for each survey.

Such a survey would start with the purpose, such as "To provide employers with prevailing wage rates so they can use competitive data to help attract and retain qualified workers and compensate them fairly."

He noted that salary surveys among law firms promote competition for lawyers. If all employers know the wage rates, there will always be some who go higher to get who they perceive to be the top attorneys.

Regarding surveys conducted by a participant in the survey, this type of activity should be reviewed on a case-by-case basis. Some companies might use a business justification for conducting a survey themselves rather than using a third party, especially for a quick and inexpensive ad hoc survey. Such surveys can be conducted without antitrust concern if it is conducted in a "pro-competitive" way. Survey participants conducting a salary survey themselves have to have a "pure mind" with regard to a "pro-competitive" survey purpose.

Attorney No. 4

This attorney offered similar opinions to the third, one of which was that future compensation plans should never be shared with peer group members. For example, if a peer asks: "what will your salaries' increase be next year?" the practitioner should answer by saying that as a matter of policy the company does not respond to those questions.

Regarding the practice of a practitioner "benchmarking" jobs against members of a peer group by calling the other companies, he said that although this activity does not seem to fit within the safety zone, it would not necessarily be anticompetitive so long as the data did not result in an agreement regarding wages or benefits and could not affect the company's prices and competitive position.

On the other side of this situation is the practitioner who receives a phone call from another company asking about salary and benefits information for a particular position so that the other company can benchmark that position. Providing this information, in the view of this attorney, does not create liability unless the results can be used for anticompetitive purposes.

This attorney summarized by saying that operating inside the guidelines always is best, but operating outside is not necessarily a problem if it is done "pro-competitively."

SUMMARY

SUMMARY

Antitrust

- Proponents of antitrust legislation indicate it is necessary to preserve competition and protect consumers.
- Critics contend that antitrust laws merely shield smaller and less efficient businesses from their larger competitors, at the expense of consumers, and that they are based on flawed economic assumptions and are a destroyer of free markets and property rights.
- Regardless of whether we like it, antitrust is here to stay for a while.

Safe Harbor

- Safe Harbor originally was promulgated for health care only, but has since been adopted by various companies in other industries.
- Operating within Safe Harbor will not be challenged by DOJ or FTC, absent extraordinary circumstances. Operating outside of Safe Harbor is not illegal, as long as it is pro-competitive and not anti-competitive. The terms "extraordinary circumstances," "pro-competitive" and "anti-competitive" are not defined.
- Conforming to the Safe Harbor requirements of a third party would preclude surveys conducted by participants.
- Conforming to the Safe Harbor requirements of three-month-old data makes "evergreen" surveys less useful.
- Conforming to the Safe Harbor requirement of a minimum number of matches for a job can preclude obtaining market information for specialized jobs.
- Conforming to the Safe Harbor requirement of dominance may distort data in an unpredictable manner for weighted averages and percentiles, and can create false or misleading market information upon which compensation decisions may be based.

Survey Practices of Practitioners

- Few companies have written guidelines about participating in or using surveys; more than one-third have informal guidelines and more than half have none whatsoever.

- More than one-third of companies require a minimum number of matches for a job to participate in or use a third-party survey. In these cases, the predominant number of matches required is five.

- About one-fourth to one-third of companies requires a maximum dominance for a job to participate in or use a third-party survey. In these cases, the predominant percentages are 25 percent, 30 percent and 35 percent.

- More than 60 percent of companies participate in non-third-party surveys (i.e., those conducted by a company acting as both a survey participant and data collector).

- Most ad-hoc, non-third-party surveys have fewer than 10 jobs.

- More than one-third of annual non-third-party surveys have more than 20 jobs.

- Most respondents have heard of the Safe Harbor guidelines, but only about one-sixth are "very familiar" with them.

Survey Practices of Consulting Firms

- There are a variety of surveys and survey practices, which complicates conforming to the Safe Harbor guidelines.

- A slight majority of firms report results with only three companies matching. The rest require five as a minimum.

- Half of the responding firms have no internal policies regarding dominance. The requirements for those that do vary from 25 percent to 33.3 percent. In any event, some surveys have their own dominance rules, such as 25 percent or 35 percent.

- Sometimes the dominance rules are enforced for cuts of the data.

- Most responding firms estimate that only a few percent of their jobs have three or four companies matching. For an individual survey of highly specialized jobs, as much as 40 percent of the jobs could have only three or four companies matching.

- The estimates of the proportion of jobs that had a company submit more than 25 percent of the data ranged from zero percent to 40 percent, with the predominant estimate being 10 percent.
- Dominance is more of an issue with smaller surveys, especially surveys conducted for industry groups. For an individual survey of an industry group, there could be as much as 85 percent of the jobs with at least one company with more than 25 percent of the data.
- Evergreen surveys tend to not conform to the three-month-old data requirements of Safe Harbor guidelines.

Attorneys' Views

- Some attorneys advise staying within Safe Harbor guidelines.
- Some attorneys say it is all right to go outside of Safe Harbor, but to act "pro-competitively," not acting collusively or discussing future data.
- The decision to comply with Safe Harbor guidelines is a balance between the need for accurate information for compensation decisions and the potential risks of running afoul of antitrust. Different attorneys are at different places along this continuum.

NEXT STEPS

NEXT STEPS

Regardless of whether one agrees with antitrust or the Safe Harbor guidelines, both are part of the compensation environment in which professionals today have to work. The statistical problems created by conformance to the guidelines may make practitioners feel as though they are doing a disservice to their company. Furthermore, though the Safe Harbor guidelines were created specifically for the health care industry, it seems possible that the government will expand the Safe Harbor notions to more — and perhaps all — industries over time.

So what should a company do? Where along the continuum of Safe Harbor guidelines is appropriate? Consider the following steps to help make an informed decision that's right for your organization:

- Educate yourself, executives, corporate counsel and/or attorneys with the information offered in this study. Do not make a decision based on incomplete information, rumors or what someone else is doing.

- Review which statistics are important in your market analysis. This is related to the compensation philosophy and knowledge of the surveys being used.

- Consider creating guidelines, rather than a hard and fast rule for all situations.

- Decide what you will do, if anything, about:
    - Participating in/using third-party surveys
    - Participating in/using non-third-party surveys
    - Age of data and evergreen surveys
    - Minimum number of companies matching
    - Maximum dominance by any one company
    - Type and currency (history, current, future) of information exchanged
    - What is done with such information
    - Discussions with the competition (phone, meetings, e-mail)

- Decide if the above considerations will apply to all surveys or just certain ones.
- Decide if you want a written policy.
- Decide how you will know such a policy is being followed.
- Ensure that the people who need to know about the policy are educated and trained in it.

Taking these steps will help to make better and informed survey policy decisions based on the facts and a broad knowledge of the history and details of Safe Harbor guidelines. You will be making conscious decisions to achieve the proper balance for your organization between the need for valid information and the potential risks of antitrust actions.

REFERENCES

References

1 www.infoplease.com/ce6/history/A0844878.html or www.bartleby.com/65/sh/ShermanA.html.

2 Fisher, Garry D. "Salary surveys — an antitrust perspective," *Personnel Administrator*, April 1985.

3 Ibid.

4 Shea, Michael B., "Decrees Offer Survey Guidelines," *ACA News*, June 1994, Volume 37, Number 6.

5 Shea, Michael B., "Antitrust Implications in the Salary Survey Process," *2003-2004 Survey Handbook and Directory: A Guide to Pay and Benefits Solutions*, WorldatWork, 2002.

6 Sixel, L.M. "Like Price Fixing, Wage Fixing Illegal," *Houston Chronicle*, Nov. 15, 2001.
Also at http://www.chron.com/cs/CDA/story.hts/business/sixel/1134720.

7 http://www.jpml.uscourts.gov/Pending_MDLs/Antitrust/MDL-1471/mdl-1471.html.

8 http://www.ca2.uscourts.gov. Search for Docket 01-7091.

9 http://www.usdoj.gov/atr/public/guidelines/0000.htm.

10 Davis, John H. *Sound Compensation Practices: A Theoretical Foundation*, Davis Consulting, Richardson, Texas. 1992.

11 Davis, John H. Distribution of Salary Survey Data Private study 2000.

12 Davis, John H. and WorldatWork, *Salary Survey Practices*, a Web-based survey, 2002.

13 As a statistical note, the percentages displayed in charts and tables may not add to 100% due to rounding.

14 Davis, John H. and Koechel, Janet F. "Fundamentals of Salary Surveys" in *2003-2004 Salary Survey Handbook & Directory: A Guide to Pay and Benefits Solutions*, Scottsdale, WorldatWork, 2002.

15 Trochim, William M. "Reliability and Validity" in Research Methods Knowledge Base, Cornell University, 2002 at http://trochim.human.cornell.edu/kb/rel&val.htm.

APPENDICES

APPENDIX 1: SAFE HARBOR GUIDELINES 74
APPENDIX 2: SHERMAN ANTITRUST ACT 79
APPENDIX 3: CONFLICTING
VIEWS OF ANTITRUST 82

APPENDIX 1:
SAFE HARBOR GUIDELINES

Safe Harbor Guidelines

In August 1996 the Department of Justice (DOJ) and the Federal Trade Commission (FTC) issued rather voluminous Statements of Antitrust Enforcement Policy in Health Care. These were first promulgated in September 1993, and have been revised since then. Below are extracted the Table of Contents to give an overview, and Statement 6 which pertains to salary and benefits surveys. (1)

**Statements of
Antitrust Enforcement Policy
in Health Care**

Issued by the
**U.S. Department of Justice
and the
Federal Trade Commission**

August 1996

TABLE OF CONTENTS

Introduction 1

Statement 1 - Mergers Among Hospitals 8

Statement 2 - Hospital Joint Ventures Involving High Technology Or Other Expensive Health Care Equipment 12

Statement 3 - Hospital Joint Ventures Involving Specialized Clinical Or Other Expensive Health Care Services 31

Statement 4 - Providers' Collective Provision Of Non-Fee-Related Information To Purchasers Of Health Care Services 40

Statement 5 - Providers' Collective Provision Of Fee-Related Information To Purchasers Of Health Care Services 43

Statement 6 - Provider Participation In Exchanges
Of Price And Cost Information 49

Statement 7 - Joint Purchasing Arrangements
Among Health Care Providers 53

Statement 8 - Physician Network Joint Ventures 61

Statement 9 - Multiprovider Networks 106

6. STATEMENT OF DEPARTMENT OF JUSTICE AND FEDERAL TRADE COMMISSION ENFORCEMENT POLICY ON PROVIDER PARTICIPATION IN EXCHANGES OF PRICE AND COST INFORMATION

Introduction

Participation by competing providers in surveys of prices for health care services, or surveys of salaries, wages or benefits of personnel, does not necessarily raise antitrust concerns. In fact, such surveys can have significant benefits for health care consumers. Providers can use information derived from price and compensation surveys to price their services more competitively and to offer compensation that attracts highly qualified personnel. Purchasers can use price survey information to make more informed decisions when buying health care services. Without appropriate safeguards, however, information exchanges among competing providers may facilitate collusion or otherwise reduce competition on prices or compensation, resulting in increased prices, or reduced quality and availability of health care services. A collusive restriction on the compensation paid to health care employees, for example, could adversely affect the availability of health care personnel.

This statement sets forth an antitrust safety zone that describes exchanges of price and cost information among providers that will not be challenged by the Agencies under the antitrust laws, absent extraordinary circumstances. It also briefly describes the Agencies' antitrust analysis of information exchanges that fall outside the antitrust safety zone.

A. Antitrust Safety Zone: Exchanges Of Price And Cost Information Among Providers That Will Not Be Challenged, Absent Extraordinary Circumstances, By The Agencies

The Agencies will not challenge, absent extraordinary circumstances, provider participation in written surveys of (a) prices for health care services, or (b) wages, salaries, or benefits of health care personnel, if the following conditions are satisfied:

1. The survey is managed by a third-party (e.g., a purchaser, government agency, health care consultant, academic institution, or trade association);

2. The information provided by survey participants is based on data more than 3 months old; and

3. There are at least five providers reporting data upon which each disseminated statistic is based, no individual provider's data represents more than 25 percent on a weighted basis of that statistic, and any information disseminated is sufficiently aggregated such that it would not allow recipients to identify the prices charged or compensation paid by any particular provider.

The conditions that must be met for an information exchange among providers to fall within the antitrust safety zone are intended to ensure that an exchange of price or cost data is not used by competing providers for discussion or coordination of provider prices or costs. They represent a careful balancing of a provider's individual interest in obtaining information useful in adjusting the prices it charges or the wages it pays in response to changing market conditions against the risk that the exchange of such information may permit competing providers to communicate with each other regarding a mutually acceptable level of prices for health care services or compensation for employees.

B. The Agencies' Analysis of Provider Exchanges Of Information That Fall Outside The Antitrust Safety Zone

Exchanges of price and cost information that fall outside the antitrust safety zone generally will be evaluated to determine whether the information exchange may have an anticompetitive effect that outweighs any procompetitive justification for the exchange. Depending on the circumstances, public, non-provider initiated surveys may not raise competitive concerns. Such surveys could allow purchasers to have useful information that they can use for procompetitive purposes (emphasis in original).

Exchanges of future prices for provider services or future compensation of employees are very likely to be considered anticompetitive. If an exchange among competing providers of price or cost information results in an agreement among competitors as to the prices for health care services or the wages to be paid to health care employees, that agreement will be considered unlawful per se.

Competing providers that are considering participating in a survey of price or cost information and are unsure of the legality of their conduct under the antitrust laws can take advantage of the Department's expedited business review procedure announced on December 1, 1992 (58 Fed. Reg. 6132 [1993]) or the Federal Trade Commission's advisory opinion procedure contained at 16 C.F.R. §§ 1.1-1.4 (1993). The Agencies will respond to a business review or advisory opinion request on behalf of providers who are considering participating in a survey of price or cost information within 90 days after all necessary information is submitted. The Department's December 1, 1992, announcement contains specific guidance as to the information that should be submitted.

Speech Referring to Safe Harbor

On August 5, 1997, Robert F. Leibenluft, Assistant Director, Bureau of Competition, Federal Trade Commission, presented a talk to the American Bar Association 1997 Annual Meeting, Section of Antitrust Law. The title of his talk was "Government Enforcement and Guidance in Health Care Antitrust: Maintaining the Balance." (2)

Referring to the consent order that created the antitrust safety zones. he said:

> Thus, I urge you to exercise caution in using a consent order as a specific guide to conduct by persons not covered by the order. Orders should be read in context, including the complaint and the analysis. Moreover, order provisions should not be read as a strict "cookbook" guide to conduct. In many cases, the order language may be more restrictive than what the law requires of others; in a few cases, following the letter of an order may not shield conduct that in a different context could violate the law.

This says that persons not in the health care provider industry should be cautious in using this as a guide for their actions, in addition to emphasizing Section B of Statement 6.

However, keep in mind that speeches do not have the authority of law. Furthermore, because of the doctrine of sovereign immunity, government officials and employees are not legally responsible for their talks or actions (i.e., you can't sue them when they are acting "officially"). But at least this talk is in concert with the published statement.

References

1. http://www.usdoj.gov/atr/public/guidelines/0000.htm
2. http://www.ftc.gov/speeches/other/aba897.htm

APPENDIX 2: SHERMAN ANTITRUST ACT

The Sherman Antitrust Act is relatively brief, and is reproduced below. (1)

The Sherman Antitrust Act (1890)

Section 1. Trusts, etc., in restraint of trade illegal; penalty

Every contract, combination in the form of trust or otherwise, or conspiracy, in restraint of trade or commerce among the several States, or with foreign nations, is declared to be illegal. Every person who shall make any contract or engage in any combination or conspiracy hereby declared to be illegal shall be deemed guilty of a felony, and, on conviction thereof, shall be punished by fine not exceeding $10,000,000 if a corporation, or, if any other person, $350,000, or by imprisonment not exceeding three years, or by both said punishments, in the discretion of the court.

Section 2. Monopolizing trade a felony; penalty

Every person who shall monopolize, or attempt to monopolize, or combine or conspire with any other person or persons, to monopolize any part of the trade or commerce among the several States, or with foreign nations, shall be deemed guilty of a felony, and, on conviction thereof, shall be punished by fine not exceeding $10,000,000 if a corporation, or, if any other person, $350,000, or by imprisonment not exceeding three years, or by both said punishments, in the discretion of the court.

Section 3. Trusts in Territories or District of Columbia illegal; combination a felony

Every contract, combination in form of trust or otherwise, or conspiracy, in restraint of trade or commerce in any Territory of the United States or of the District of Columbia, or in restraint of trade or commerce between any such Territory and another, or between any such Territory or Territories and any State or States or the District of Columbia, or with foreign nations, or between the District of Columbia and any State or States or foreign nations, is declared illegal. Every person who shall make any such contract or engage in any such combination or conspiracy, shall be deemed guilty of a felony, and, on conviction thereof, shall be punished by fine not exceeding $10,000,000 if a corporation, or, if any other person, $350,000, or by imprisonment not exceeding three years, or both said punishments, in the discretion of the court.

Section 4. Jurisdiction of courts; duty of United States attorneys; procedure

The several district courts of the United States are invested with jurisdiction to prevent and restrain violations of sections 1 to 7 of this title; and it shall be the duty of the several United States attorneys, in their respective districts, under the direction of the Attorney General, to institute proceedings in equity to prevent and restrain such violations. Such proceedings may be by way of petition setting forth the case and praying that such violation shall be enjoined or otherwise prohibited. When the parties complained of shall have been duly notified of such petition the court shall proceed, as soon as may be, to the hearing and determination of the case; and pending such petition and before final decree, the court may at any time make such temporary restraining order or prohibition as shall be deemed just in the premises.

Section 5. Bringing in additional parties

Whenever it shall appear to the court before which any proceeding under section 4 of this title may be pending, that the ends of justice require that other parties should be brought before the court, the court may cause them to be summoned, whether they reside in the district in which the court is held or not; and subpoenas to that end may be served in any district by the marshal thereof.

Section 6. Forfeiture of property in transit

Any property owned under any contract or by any combination, or pursuant to any conspiracy (and being the subject thereof) mentioned in section 1 of this title, and being in the course of transportation from one State to another, or to a foreign country, shall be forfeited to the United States, and may be seized and condemned by like proceedings as those provided by law for the forfeiture, seizure, and condemnation of property imported into the United States contrary to law.

Section 6a. Conduct involving trade or commerce with foreign nations

Sections 1 to 7 of this title shall not apply to conduct involving trade or commerce (other than import trade or import commerce) with foreign nations unless:

(1) such conduct has a direct, substantial, and reasonably foreseeable effect

(A) on trade or commerce which is not trade or commerce with foreign nations, or on import trade or import commerce with foreign nations; or

(B) on export trade or export commerce with foreign nations, of a person engaged in such trade or commerce in the United States; and

(2) such effect gives rise to a claim under the provisions of sections 1 to 7 of this title, other than this section.

If sections 1 to 7 of this title apply to such conduct only because of the operation of paragraph (1)(B), then sections 1 to 7 of this title shall apply to such conduct only for injury to export business in the United States.

Section 7. "Person" or "persons" defined

The word "person," or "persons," wherever used in sections 1 to 7 of this title shall be deemed to include corporations and associations existing under or authorized by the laws of either the United States, the laws of any of the Territories, the laws of any State, or the laws of any foreign country.

References

1. http://www.stolaf.edu/people/becker/antitrust/statutes/sherman.html

Also http://www.stolaf.edu/people/simmonsr/sherman.html

APPENDIX 3: CONFLICTING VIEWS OF ANTITRUST

During the research for this study, it became apparent that there are strong, conflicting views on antitrust. Virtually since its inception, antitrust has been controversial. Proponents have seen it as a preserver of competition and a protector of consumers, while critics have viewed it as based on flawed economic assumptions and a destroyer of free markets and property rights. Where does the truth lie?

Following are presented highlights of the views of antitrust supporters and antitrust critics. This will serve as an introduction to the rewards practitioner who wants to delve further into these laws that are increasingly impacting salary surveys. Several references are given to aid those who want to inquire further, to enable them to reach their own conclusions about antitrust.

General Views of Supporters

- The historic goal of the antitrust laws is to protect economic freedom and opportunity by promoting free and open competition in the marketplace.
- Combinations, trusts, and monopolies tend to restrict output, and thus drive up prices.
- Antitrust prohibits business practices that unreasonably deprive consumers of the benefits of competition, resulting in higher prices for inferior products and services.
- Antitrust laws protect competition.
- Antitrust laws protect consumers.
- Certain agreements and exchanges of information between competitors are bad.
- Antitrust laws preserve economic freedom and our free-enterprise system.

General Views of Critics

- The Sherman Antitrust Act was never intended to protect competition as such. It was a protectionist act designed to shield smaller and less efficient businesses from their larger competitors, all at the expense of consumers.
- Breaking up large companies and preventing mergers damages the free market and raises prices for consumers.
- Only government, not private business, can create monopolies and legal barriers to entry.
- Antitrust violates property rights and destroys economic freedom.
- Antitrust is immoral, as it punishes the successful for being successful.
- Antitrust laws are fluid, non-objective, and often retroactive, punishing a company for an action that was not legally defined as a crime at time of its commission.
- Antitrust is based on a static and unrealistic view of the market.
- A narrow definition of the "relevant market" can make any firm a "monopolist."
- Antitrust law is wielded by business rivals and their allies in the political arena.

Lack of space prevents providing details that support each point made. However, a few examples will be given to illustrate the nature of the discussion.

Examples of Views of Supporters

The general view of supporters is that antitrust laws preserve competition and protect consumers. Three examples are given here.

The Federal Trade Commission Web site has a 16-page electronic booklet titled "Promoting Competition, Protecting Consumers: A Plain English Guide to Antitrust Law" (1) In its preface, it states ...

The FTC is a consumer protection agency with two mandates under the FTC Act: to guard the marketplace from unfair methods of competition, and to prevent unfair or deceptive acts or practices that harm consumers. These tasks often involve the analysis of complex business practices and economic issues. When the Commission succeeds in doing both its jobs, it protects consumer sovereignty — the freedom to choose goods and services in an open marketplace at a price and quality that fit the consumer's needs — and fosters opportunity for businesses by ensuring a level playing field among competitors. In pursuing its work, the FTC can file cases in both federal court and a special administrative forum.

> ..."*Antitrust laws ... are the Magna Carta of free enterprise. They are as important to the preservation of economic freedom and our free-enterprise system as the Bill of Rights is to the protection of our fundamental personal freedoms.*"
>
> — The Supreme Court, United States v. Topco Associates, Inc. 1972 [Italics in original]

A Department of Justice website (2) gives an overview of its antitrust Division. An extract on the goal of antitrust is:

> The historic goal of the antitrust laws is to protect economic freedom and opportunity by promoting competition in the marketplace. Competition in a free market benefits American consumers through lower prices, better quality and greater choice. Competition provides businesses the opportunity to compete on price and quality, in an open market and on a level playing field, unhampered by anticompetitive restraints. Competition also tests and hardens American companies at home, the better to succeed abroad.

This website links to another (3) which goes into more detail of the DOJ view of antitrust.

> Many consumers have never heard of antitrust laws, but when these laws are effectively and responsibly enforced, they can save consumers millions and even billions of dollars a year in illegal overcharges. Most states have antitrust laws, and so does the federal government. Essentially, these laws prohibit business practices that unreasonably deprive consumers of the benefits of competition, resulting in higher prices for inferior products and services.
>
> Antitrust laws protect competition. Free and open competition benefits consumers by ensuring lower prices and new and better products. In a freely competitive market, each competing business generally will try to attract consumers by cutting its prices and increasing the quality of its products or services. Competition and the profit opportunities it brings also stimulate businesses to find new, innovative and more efficient methods of production.

Consumers benefit from competition through lower prices and better products and services. Companies that fail to understand or react to consumer needs may soon find themselves losing out in the competitive battle. When competitors agree to fix prices, rig bids or allocate (divide up) customers, consumers lose the benefits of competition. The prices that result when competitors agree in these ways are artificially high; such prices do not accurately reflect cost and therefore distort the allocation of society's resources. The result is a loss not only to U.S. consumers and taxpayers, but also the U.S. economy.

When the competitive system is operating effectively, there is no need for government intrusion. The law recognizes that certain arrangements between firms — such as competitors cooperating to perform joint research and development projects — may benefit consumers by allowing the firms that have reached the agreement to compete more effectively against other firms. The law does not condemn all agreements between companies, only those that threaten to raise prices to consumers or to deprive them of new and better products.

But when competing firms get together to fix prices, to rig bids, to divide business between them or to make other anticompetitive arrangements that provide no benefits to consumers, the government will act promptly to protect the interests of American consumers.

Two additional references give similar views. The Legal Information Institute, a non-profit activity of Cornell Law School, gives an overview of antitrust. (4) The American Management Association, in one of its guidebooks for managers, gives a similar view (5, page 3).

These views are all consistent, saying that the antitrust laws preserve competition and protect consumers.

Examples of Views of Critics

The general view of critics is that antitrust is based on flawed economic assumptions and is a destroyer of free markets and property rights. They maintain that a free-market economy, based on voluntary exchange, is the only economic system consistent with human liberty, whereas antitrust introduces coercion in the economy and violates the property rights of the parties in their business transactions.

Brief examples are given concerning the origins of antitrust and of its consequences.

Origins of antitrust

The late nineteenth century was a period of great economic expansion, fostered in part by new technology. Supplies of agricultural and industrial products expanded and prices declined in general. DiLorenzo describes the general economic climate (6) [p 2-6] and adds.

> In introducing federal antitrust legislation, Sen. Sherman and his congressional allies claimed that combinations or trusts tended to restrict output and thus drove up prices.
>
> However, prices in these industries were falling. According to Henderson (7)
>
> The price of steel fell 53 percent, refined sugar 22 percent, lead 12 percent, and zinc 20 percent. ... between 1880 and 1890 the output of petroleum products rose 393 percent and the price fell 61 percent. These findings turn the conventional wisdom on its head. ... The oil trust did not charge high prices because it had 90 percent of the market. It got 90 percent of the refined oil market by charging low prices.
>
> Many supporters [of antitrust laws] were farmers upset about the low prices they got for their crops, others were small businesspeople who couldn't compete. Many trustbusters in Congress recognized that the low prices that came about because of the trusts enhanced the consumers' well being.

The real reason behind antitrust is illustrated by this statement during the House debates over the Sherman Act by Congressman William Mason, who stated (8)

> "Trusts have made products cheaper, have reduced prices; but if the price of oil, for instance, were reduced to one cent a barrel, it would not right the wrong done to the people of this country by the 'trusts' which have destroyed legitimate competition and driven honest men from legitimate business enterprises."

In other words, critics say that antitrust was an attack on the success of large efficient industries that got that way because consumers favored their products and prices. Mason and his colleagues favored antitrust laws because the low prices of bigger companies were driving out the smaller, less-efficient competitors.

In summary, critics maintain the Sherman Antitrust Act was never intended to protect competition as such. It was a protectionist act designed to shield smaller and less efficient businesses from their larger competitors, all at the expense of consumers.

Some consequences of antitrust

Critics give examples of high-profile antitrust cases that illustrate their points. Three cases are mentioned here.

Standard Oil

Kitner and Bast (9) and Grant (10) go into great detail on this famous case. Armentano summarizes it as (11):

> For example, in the classic Standard Oil case (1911), it is still widely believed that Standard of New Jersey was convicted because it had restricted production, raised prices, and engaged in ruthless predatory practices to destroy competition. Yet none of this was ever proven at court. Standard lost the decision in 1911 because a lower court in 1909 had determined that the formation of its holding company in 1899 was prima facie illegal since it ended the potentiality of competition between the (now) merged firms. The Supreme Court, while announcing a rule of reason, simply reaffirmed the unanalytical decision of that lower court.

> An objective study of the petroleum industry between 1859 and 1911 would reveal that Standard did not plunder consumers or competitors. The price of kerosene — the industry's major product — dropped from over 50 cents a gallon in the early 1860s to less than six cents in the late 1890s. While Standard always did a large share of the industry's business, they always had competition. When they were dissolved in 1911 for monopolizing in restraint of trade, there were at least 147 independent petroleum refining companies selling products in competition with the Standard Oil Company. The industry was not monopolized.

Alcoa

Kitner and Bast (9) again give details, alleging that Alcoa did nothing wrong. Greenspan is more scathing of the Alcoa decision. (12)

> [P 70] Those who allege that the purpose of the antitrust laws is to protect competition, enterprise, and efficiency, need to be reminded of the following quotation from Judge Learned Hand's indictment of ALCOA's so-called monopolistic practices.

> "It was not inevitable that it should always anticipate increases in the

demand for ingot and be prepared to supply them. Nothing compelled it to keep doubling and redoubling its capacity before others entered the field. It insists that it never excluded competitors; but we can think of no more effective exclusion than progressively to embrace each new opportunity as it opened, and to face every newcomer with new capacity already geared into a great organization, having the advantage of experience, trade connections and the elite of personnel."

ALCOA was condemned for being too successful, too efficient, and too good a competitor.

The effective purpose, the hidden intent, and the actual practice of the antitrust laws in the United States have led to the condemnation of the productive and efficient members of our society because they are productive and efficient.

Staples and Office Depot

Not only does the government attack what it thinks are monopolies, it also takes action to prevent what it perceives as potential monopolies, as illustrated by the attempted merger of Staples and Office Depot in 1997. Lynch describes the federal government's successful effort to block the merger of these two office supply companies. (13)

> In its efforts to block a merger between Staples and Office Depot, the Federal Trade Commission, which itself purchases office supplies from 105 vendors, had objected to this marriage on the grounds that it would result in a manila envelope monopoly.
>
> Never mind, say the regulators, that Staples and Office Depot once combined would account for roughly 6 percent of the office supply market nationwide. Never mind, they say, that both stores lower the cost of office supplies by at least 20 percent in markets in which only one enters. ... Never mind, they say, that the business strategy to which both stores owe their success is relentless price-cutting, which has saved Americans hundreds of millions of dollars since superstores first revolutionized the office supply business in the mid-1980s.
>
> The absurdity in this case ... is the FTC's contention that no other stores compete vigorously enough with Office Depot and Staples to discipline their price increasing urges. Forget the small mom-and-pop corner grocery that carries cards. The FTC claims that Wal-Mart, which already sells more office supplies than Staples and Office Depot combined, isn't a threat to the single-subject superstores. Nor are the fax order houses that deliver to

anyone. ... Worse yet, the FTC claims there is no possibility for entry into the market in the event that a monopolist does increase prices.

Principles underlying antitrust

Many commentators have discussed antitrust from the point of view of the underlying principles, concluding that antirust is immoral and irrational. Some of their points include the violation of property rights, the non-objective nature of antitrust, the unrealistic market assumptions, and the fact that only government can create monopolies, among others. Space prevents providing examples of these discussions. However, references are provided below that support these views.

In summary, antitrust is controversial. The rewards practitioner who wishes to gain a better understanding of the differing views of the antitrust laws that are impacting salary surveys has a wealth of information at hand. The references below will furnish a good starting point for that education.

Selected References Giving Supporting Views

1. http://www.ftc.gov/bc/compguide/index.htm, updated August 2002.

2. http://www.justice.gov/atr/public/div_stats/9142.htm

3. http://www.justice.gov/atr/overview.html.

4. http://www.law.cornell.edu/topics/antitrust.html.

5. Matto, Edward A. *A Manager's Guide to the Antitrust Laws*. Amacom, New York 1980.

Selected References Giving Critical Views

6. DiLorenzo, Thomas J. "The Origins of Antitrust — Rhetoric vs. Reality." *In Regulation* published by the Cato Institute, Fall 1990, v. 13, no. 3. Also at http://www.cato.org/pubs/regulation/regv13n3/reg13n3-dilorenzo.html.

7. Henderson, David R. "Of Price and Men" in *Red Herring*, June 2000. Also at http://www.herring.com/mag/issue79/mag-price-79.html.

8. Kitner, Earl. W., editor. *The Legislative History Federal Antitrust Laws and Related Statutes*. New York. Chelsea House Publishers 1978. This book contains the record of House and Senate debates on S 1 (The Sherman Act), 51st Congress, in 1890), taken from the Congressional Record.

9. Kopel, David B., and Bast, Joseph. "Antitrust's Greatest Hits" *Reason* November 2001.

10. Grant, R.W. *The Incredible Bread Machine, 2nd Edition*. San Francisco. Fox & Wilkes. 1999.

11. Armentano, D.T. "Antitrust Policy: Reform or Repeal?" In *Policy Analysis* published by the Cato Institute, Policy Analysis No. 21, January 18, 1983. Also at http://www.cato.org/pubs/pas/pa021.html

12. Greenspan, Alan. "Antitrust." In *Capitalism: The Unknown Ideal*. Edited by Ayn Rand. New York: Signet, 1967.

13. Lynch, Michael W. "Pricing Pencils, the FTC's Creative Market Definitions," *Reason* August/September 1997.

14. Boaz, David. "Chrysler, Microsoft, and Industrial Policy" *Today's Commentary*, November 8, 1996. Published by the Cato Institute. Also at http://www.cato.org/dailys/11-08-96.html

15. Rand, Ayn. "America's Persecuted Minority: Big Business." In *Capitalism: The Unknown Ideal*. Edited by Ayn Rand. New York: Signet, 1967.

16. Bork, Robert H. *Antitrust Paradox: A Policy at War with Itself*. Basic Books, New York, 1978

Selected References Discussing Underlying Principles

17. Levy, Robert A. "Antitrust" Chapter 41 of *Cato Handbook for Congress: Policy Recommendations for the 107th Congress* edited by Edward H. Crane and David Boaz published by the Cato Institute. August 2002.
Also at http://www.cato.org/pubs/handbook/handbook107.html

18. Younkins, Edward W. "Antitrust Laws Should Be Abolished" At http://www.quebecoislibre.org/000219-13.htm

19. Greenspan, Alan. "Antitrust." In *Capitalism: The Unknown Ideal*. Edited by Ayn Rand. New York: Signet, 1967.

20. Kopel, David B., and Bast, Joseph. "Antitrust's Greatest Hits" *Reason* November 2001

21. Skousen, Mark. *Economic Logic*. Washington, DC Capital Press 2000.

22. Crews Jr., Clyde Wayne. "The Antitrust Terrible 10: Why the Most Reviled 'Anti-competitive' Business Practices Can Benefit Consumers in the New Economy." In *Policy Analysis* published by the Cato Institute, Policy Analysis No. 405, June 28, 2001.
Also at http://www.cato.org/pubs/pas/pa-405es.html

23. Rand, Ayn. "America's Persecuted Minority: Big Business." In *Capitalism: The Unknown Ideal*. Edited by Ayn Rand. New York: Signet, 1967.